CAPTAIN PUCKETT

CAPTAIN PUCKETT

Sea stories of a former Panama Canal pilot

Kenneth P. Puckett
with William D. LaRue

CHESTNUT HEIGHTS
PUBLISHING

Chestnut Heights Publishing

Published by Chestnut Heights Publishing

Print ISBN 978-0-692-08611-7

Library of Congress Control Number: 2018938530

Contact Kenneth P. Puckett at panamacanalpilot.com

Contact William D. LaRue at williamlarue.com

Cover design by www.ebooklaunch.com
Front cover photo by Jonathan Ross via Shutterstock
Back cover photo by Rick Thompson

Typesetting services by BOOKOW.COM

This book is proudly dedicated to U.S. Army Chief Warrant Officer Carter C. James, who was my mentor and much more.
— Kenneth P. Puckett

Contents

Preface   1

1. Kentucky   8

2. The Queen   19

3. The Navy   27

4. George Archey   43

5. The Army   56

6. Vietnam   63

7. Japan, Korea and the Philippines   77

8. A Man. A Plan. A Canal: Panama   88

9. The apprentice   97

10. Night transits   107

11. Water buffalo   111

12. Coal ship   115

13. A hole in the gate   119

14. Russians   124

15. Salaries and bonuses   132

16. Nautical school   136

17. Living in Panama   138

18. A pooping monkey and killer bees   144

19. Chinese interpreter 148
20. Queen Elizabeth II 152
21. India Star 154
22. Blind pilot 157
23. Don't ask, don't tell 160
24. Alcohol counseling 165
25. Darlene 169
26. The invasion 174
27. Bananas 178
28. Sarah Terry 182
29. The yacht accident 185
30. The Trump Princess 187
31. Captain Puckett goes to Washington 190
33. Disney 198
34. Historic Disney cruise 206
Epilogue 216
About the authors 222

Preface

I was sitting in an airplane not long ago, flying first-class because I had an upgrade, and the passenger in the seat next to me was a gentleman in his late 80s. We got talking a bit, and he told me he had been an engineer and had worked with NASA on the Apollo space program. Then he asked me what I did for a living.

I stand on the bridge in my white pilot's uniform as the P&O Cruises' ship M/V Aurora passes through the Panama Canal in January 2016.

I told him I had been a pilot on the Panama Canal.

"You're a pilot?" he asked. "What did you fly?"

"I didn't fly anything," I said.

Now, this was a well-educated man trained in aviation, and he still didn't understand the difference between airplane pilots and maritime pilots. After he had a few drinks and fell asleep, I couldn't help but think how often over the years I encountered similar confusion when I told someone what I did for nearly 16 years on the Panama Canal. When a Minnesota newspaper ran a short item announcing I would be giving a lecture in April 2001, the headline read: "Navy pilot discusses Panama Canal."

Let me give you a brief history of maritime piloting.

Long before the dawn of aviation, pilots helped to keep waterways safe. Pilots existed way back in ancient Egypt, and they are even mentioned in the Bible: "And all that handle the oar, the mariners, and all the pilots of the sea" (Ezekiel 27:29).

By the 14th and 15th centuries, a sailing vessel coming into an area would be greeted by a guy in a rowboat or fishing boat sitting out there and saying, "Hey, I know the location of the harbor. I know the channel. I know the depth of the water. I know how the wind is going to be blowing. I'll guide you into port. I'll be your pilot."

The problem was, sometimes the pilot secretly worked for pirates, and he would deliberately run the ship aground, and the pirates would come aboard and steal everything. This method of piracy got so bad that, if a ship ran aground even accidentally, the captain would hang the pilot over the side and execute him as a warning to others.

Understandably, the legitimate pilots began to worry they were taking their lives into their own hands by helping the ships. To solve this, the pilots got together on the west coast of Europe to establish some rules and regulations. They got the kings to give them authority and a monopoly in exchange for making sure those who worked as pilots were checked out and found to be legit.

Then in 1514, the Corporation of Trinity House of England was established to regulate pilotage, and it set standards throughout the world that are still in operation today, including licensing of pilots. Today, there are about 80,000 pilots assigned to harbors, ports and canals around the world. Their job is to climb aboard arriving and departing ships to help their captains navigate waters and avoid hazards that can damage a ship, such as hidden reefs and tricky currents.

The pilots on the Panama Canal historically have been looked upon as among the best. In other places, a pilot's only responsibility might be to bring a ship through a channel into a harbor or through the mouth of a river. Panama Canal pilots are required to be channel pilots, docking pilots and locks pilots. It requires tremendous skill for them to bring a ship through a complicated set of locks, often fighting wind and currents that can send the vessel into a wall. Then they take the same ship across a man-made lake where tops of trees lurk below the surface and through a mountain range where the edge of the waterway looms feet away. Even today, with GPS and radar and other electronic aids, a Panama Canal pilot who doesn't know what he is doing can put a big cargo ship very quickly into a muddy bank.

I went to work as a Panama Canal pilot in January 1981, about four years after U.S. President Jimmy Carter and Panamanian leader Gen. Omar Torrijos signed treaties in which the United States agreed to turn over the canal to Panama at the end of 1999. At the time, I was thrilled to get the job, unaware of the extent to which I had stepped into a hornets' nest of anger, fear and bitterness among Americans living and working there. Many had called the Panama Canal Zone their home for generations. They had been living in an American Utopia with all sorts of benefits and privileges, from cheap housing to imported groceries, and now they resented the fact the treaties were taking that away.

When I arrived, I was one of 35 experienced captains recruited from across the country to replace Panama Canal pilots who had quit or retired after the treaties were signed. I was also among the half-dozen

Pilots in Training (PIT) with military backgrounds. I had served in the Navy as master, mate, navigator and senior quartermaster on numerous ocean-going vessels for more than eight years. After transferring to the Army in 1966, I served as a ship's pilot in Vietnam, Japan and South Korea. I also came under enemy fire delivering cargo on ships along the Vietnamese coast. While I was in the Army, I was trained, certified and licensed as a master/pilot and captained several vessels. When I retired from the Army in 1978, I held the rank of chief warrant officer CWO4.

I was almost 40 when I began working on the canal. Yet some longtime ship pilots resented me right away, treating me like a raw cadet. Many just didn't like military guys. They also resented that I hadn't come up through the U.S. Merchant Marine system and its good-old-boy network steeped in nepotism, which is how they got their jobs.

These guys also had a union mentality about everything, which I thought was stupid because they were employees of the federal government. I said to a pilot one day, "You can act like you are union, but forget it. All you can do is negotiate your working conditions. You're not going to negotiate your salary. And if you quit working, the federal government says, 'Goodbye.'" And that's exactly what happened in August 1981 to the air traffic controllers when President Ronald Reagan replaced them for going on strike.

I was about a year into my 19 months of training as an apprentice pilot on the Panama Canal when one morning I got a call notifying me I was going to be accompanying two senior pilots, John and Ron, for transit on the Royal Viking Sky, a 500-passenger luxury cruise ship. Only the most senior pilots were ever assigned to cruise ships because of the delicate nature of guiding them through the locks. I was thrilled because I was going to tag along and get some great training from two very experienced pilots.

The voyage also gave me another trip to fulfill the requirement I take 195 supervised transits through the canal before I could become a Step One pilot, the first level after the apprenticeship period.

When I arrived at the ready room, I spotted John and Ron waiting for a launch, a small boat that would take us from the shore across the water to the ship.

I introduced myself. "I'll be joining you for pilot training," I said.

"Look, Puckett," John told me. "We didn't ask for an apprentice pilot. You can get on the ship, but you stay away from us. It's not our job to train you." Truthfully, it was part of their jobs to train the new pilots. I'm not saying they were bad at their jobs. They were exceptional pilots, and I became good friends with both, eventually. But they didn't want to be teachers.

"Look, I have to make the transit," I said quietly. "I got to make the trip. I'll just stay out of your way. I'll watch what you do."

Pilots routinely allowed apprentices to accompany them on the bridge, observe them, and even do some ship-handling under supervision.

Not these two guys.

"We don't even want you on the bridge," Ron said.

I decided not to argue further. I would get credit for the transit whether I was on the bridge or not.

After we climbed the pilot's ladder and boarded the ship, the ship's chief officer met us at the gangway. He looked at me and the Panama Canal pilot cap I was wearing. "Why the third pilot?" he asked.

"Oh, he's the apprentice," Ron told him. "He's not even coming to the bridge."

When I got a moment alone with the officer, I told him I was the "staff pilot."

"What's that?" he asked.

"It's my job to hang out with the cruise director and help entertain the guests."

"Really?" he said. "That's pretty cool."

And just like that, I had a heck of a time during the next eight hours on the Royal Viking Sky. I hung out with the cruise director. I went to the dining rooms and had some great food. I got to visit with crew and passengers. Because I was wearing that pilot's hat, people accepted me as just part of the Panama Canal experience.

About 5 o'clock when the ship reached the other side of the canal, I rejoined the two senior pilots at the portal, where we got into another launch and headed back for the harbor. They still weren't talking to me. They were being real buggers.

Instead, they were chortling over the gifts they received from the ship's captain. In those days, when a pilot finished a transit, it was traditional for the captain to give him a "presento," often a carton of cigarettes or a bottle of fine liquor.

Ron said to John, "Did you get a bottle?"

John said, "Yeah, I got a nice bottle." He pulled a bottle of Cutty Sark, a quality Scottish whiskey, out of his pilot pack.

Then Ron pulled out a bottle of Cutty Sark, and he was pretty thrilled about it, too.

I smiled and said, "I got a bottle." I pulled out Crown Royal in a felt bag. This was a very expensive Canadian whiskey, the best of the best.

"Where'd you get that?" Ron asked.

"The cruise director gave me this bottle," I said. "But, you know something? I don't drink."

And with that, I turned and threw the bottle into the water.

Ron and John flipped out.

"Why'd you do that? We would have taken it," Ron said.

"Why should I give it to you guys?" I said. "You wouldn't talk to me all day. You don't want me on the bridge. So, to heck with you."

I wasn't finished. As we pulled into shore, I looked at John and said, "Let me tell you something. I'm a 40-year-old apprentice pilot. I can handle that. But I got the same first name as you do."

And without saying more, I got off the launch and went ashore before they could respond. John and Ron had their own government car to take them home. I got in another car by myself.

About a week later I was back in the ready room getting prepared to go on another transit when John came in.

He came right over to me.

He said, "I've been looking for you, Puckett. Your name is Kenneth. It's not John. You don't have the same first name as me."

I said, "Yes, I do. My name is 'Captain,' just like you. And I expect you from now on to treat me like it. If you want me to respect you, you should at least respect me."

And as I walked out, other pilots started laughing and saying, "Hey, John! He got you."

I was only an apprentice at the time, but it was my nature to stick up for myself. It's always hard for a person with my personality to let things like that go. What John and Ron did snubbing me on the cruise ship wasn't so bad. A lot of senior pilots busted your chops if you were an apprentice. I'd had worse.

While other apprentices at the time didn't say anything when treated with a lack of respect, I was different. I grew up in a rural part of northern Kentucky in the 1940s and 1950s. We weren't dirt poor, but we were poor enough. We were like many people in the South who didn't have much, but if you crossed them, they might come after you. You threatened their pride and you might get shot.

The attitude I developed growing up was: Don't mess with me. I had pride. Sometimes, pride was the only thing I had.

1. Kentucky

I remember the day I was told my father was dead. It was in January 1945, amid the most frigid part of winter. I was just 3 years old. My mother, my younger brother, Ron, and I were living in a small place along a dirt road in the northern Kentucky community of Cold Spring. It was so rural we only got our mail once or twice a week. That day, a car drove up the road and stopped at our home. Out stepped a guy in Army uniform. He came to our door and handed my mother a telegram. I don't know exactly what it said, and I was too young to ask, but I remember my mother fell to pieces. She would then quietly explain that my father, Sgt. Nute Puckett, had been killed by the Japanese while fighting overseas in World War II. He was just 22 years old.

He had been away from home during most of the war years, and so I have few memories of him, other than of a pleasant, soft-spoken man with a wide smile. He had been born James Newton "Nute" Puckett on July 2, 1922, in Irvine, Kentucky, a small community along the Kentucky River. Census records show he had at least six brothers and sisters. His father, also named James, was a farmer.

On September 28, 1940, two months after turning 18, Nute signed up for the U.S. Army infantry at Fort Thomas, a military post located about five miles from Cold Spring. Enlistment records show he had a grammar school education, and he was a bit on the small size at just under 5 feet 6 inches tall and weighing 137 pounds.

After he was promoted to sergeant, he was sent to the Philippines in early 1945 with the 161st Infantry Regiment to help liberate the nation from Japanese occupation. On January 18, 1945, while leading a scouting party to clear out remnants of the Japanese in Luzon, a sniper shot him dead. The Army buried him right there in the Philippines, where his remains rested until 1949, when his mother, Ida, ordered a government gravestone and had him brought home to be interred in the Puckett family plot in Kentucky.

As far as I know, my mother never had any contact with the Puckett side of the family after he died. I know I never did. However, while growing up, in good times and bad times, I held onto one certainty: I was proud to be the son of Sgt. Nute Puckett, a hero who died fighting for his country in World War II.

My mom was born Vernice Vogt on April 26, 1920, in Campbell, Kentucky, the third of four children. Her father, Charles, was employed for a time as a factory shoemaker. Then he and my grandmother, Amelia, separated due to him drinking and raising hell on the Ohio River. I understand he lost everything a couple of times due to gambling. After they split, Grandma Vogt raised their kids in a tiny bungalow in Highland Heights, Kentucky, while working as a factory seamstress making uniforms for the military.

My mother gave birth to me March 24, 1941, in Highland Heights, which at the time was dotted with little truck farms along U.S. Route 25, a highway that runs south all the way into Tennessee. I was delivered by a midwife, who also happened to be the local veterinarian, of all things.

I was born in the same bungalow in which Mom was raised by my grandmother. The home was pretty much a shack. It had only two rooms and an outhouse – a "three-holer," as we used to call it. You could go in and sit with your grandma and grandpa. They later added third and fourth rooms to the house, but the place didn't have an indoor toilet until I was 12 or 13.

When my mother became a widow, she had little more than a small life insurance payout to make ends meet. In October 1945, just a few months after being widowed, she married Clarence C. Combs, an

Army master sergeant who was 36 at the time. In 1947, she gave birth to their only child together, my half-sister, Barbara Sue.

My stepfather remained in the Army after World War II and received assignments that took our family to many different places, including two years at Fort Knox when I was in the fourth and fifth grades. We lived for a while in the city of Fort Thomas, which was named after the Army base that existed there until 1964. The city sits on a cliff just above Brent, Kentucky, where ferry boats during the summer transported passengers across the Ohio River to Coney Island of Ohio amusement park and adjoining horseracing track.

We also lived for a time down the river in Newport, Kentucky, which had several big breweries and was a major railroad hub. The city was home to many disabled guys who had lost arms or legs after falling off trains. Some who had railroad pensions lived together in a five-story building. In the summer they often would hang out of the windows and use a rope, with a fish hook attached, to lower a pail in which they placed a nickel, dime or quarter.

"Hey, kid, go get me some beer," one would say to me. I grabbed the pail and headed for one of the breweries, which would fill the pail with beer. The breweries did this without charge for these disabled men. I got to keep the nickel, dime or quarter for my trouble.

My mother arranged for me to live with Grandma Vogt in Highland Heights from first to fourth grades, rather than pulling me in and out of schools whenever she moved. My mother registered me in school as "Kenneth Combs" and my brother as "Ronald Combs," even though our stepfather never adopted us. It was typical Southern rural mentality for her to do this. I guess she didn't want people gossiping why her two boys had different last names from their parents.

I think I had a very good attitude in those days, despite our unsettled lives. Nothing seemed to faze me. I was lucky to have grandparents who loved me deeply and helped to take care of me in times when my mother couldn't.

I was baptized Protestant and went to a Protestant church each Sunday. My mother was Protestant as was her mother. But right after I was born, Grandpa Vogt's mother, who was known as Grandma Cinni, was adamant about me being baptized Catholic. Without telling my mother, she sneaked me down to her Catholic Church and got me baptized there. After a relative told me about this years later, I liked to tell people, "All I have to do now is to find a rabbi and I'm fully covered."

Besides being very religious, Grandma Vogt was a real patriot before, during and after World War II. She used to say to me, "We're American Germans, not German Germans." When I was a toddler, during the war years, she made little U.S. Army and U.S. Navy uniforms for me to wear. The Army one was very authentic, pretty much right down to the letter; she took a pair of Army khaki pants she got from the factory to make it. The Navy uniform was somewhat different from the real thing, but it was still impressive. At other times, she worked in a factory that made suits for very wealthy men in northern Kentucky and in Cincinnati. She could just look at them and tell their suit size.

After Grandpa Vogt died in 1949, my grandmother became Grandma Collins when she married James Collins, a quiet, hard-working man who repaired small diesel engines used on boats that traveled up and down the Ohio River. He also fixed industrial sewing machines, which is probably how he met my grandmother.

Grandpa and Grandma Collins owned a little farm that grew tomatoes and other produce. They'd load the produce on the back of a small truck and drive to the Cincinnati side of the river to sell at markets there.

I was very close to Grandpa Collins, who spoke English with a thick German accent. Although he was my step-grandfather, he treated me like I was his flesh and blood. He was just the nicest man to me. But he was also a tough old dude, and he looked it, too. My God, he had

That's me as a toddler in the early 1940s, posing in Army and Navy uniforms that
Grandma Vogt made for me by hand.

a lot of tattoos. He was tattooed from his ankles to his neck. I never
have seen so many tattoos.

I was told that Grandpa Collins served on a submarine with the
German Navy in World War I and that he was captured by the British
and turned over to the Americans, who shipped him to a POW camp
in the United States. One day he and another POW walked off and
never went back to the camp. One reason I think there's some truth to
this story is that, whenever government people came anywhere near
his home, Grandpa Collins would kind of disappear.

One other thing I remember about him and Grandma: Each was
only about 4-foot-10. They were so tiny they slept sideways on the
little hide-a-bed they had at home. When I stayed there, I used to
sleep next to them on a cot.

I remember Mom from those days as a very, very beautiful and highly intelligent woman who used to sit down and do the New York Times Sunday crossword puzzles in ink and never miss a lick. But after being widowed, she developed a drinking problem that only worsened with time. I can remember her doing the puzzles with a pen in one hand and a beer in the other.

As the years passed, she began spending more and more time in the taverns. In those days I didn't realize she was an alcoholic. I didn't even know what that term meant then. I know now she was just one of those people who can't have even one drink without it becoming a problem. I believe she picked up the gene for alcoholism from her father. As it did him, alcohol took the best of her. She had a strong temper that only got worse when she drank, which meant there were times she would grab us children and physically beat us.

By the time I entered my teen years, she was deteriorating quickly from the effects of drinking. But I couldn't change that. I just tried to have a positive attitude.

In 1953, when I was in the eighth grade, Clarence Combs apparently decided it was all too much for him to take. He had Type 1 diabetes, and the situation with my mother wasn't working out too well for him. He was a decent man. He was always nice to me. But he just got up one day, went to the veterans hospital and then walked away from the family. He deserted us. I know that sounds harsh, but he left behind three children who needed a father. I never saw him again. He left my mother with a meager military retirement check, which was $85 or $95 a month.

After that, our whole way of life collapsed. I ended back with my grandparents again. When I wasn't with them – such as on the weekends or when I wasn't working – I would stay with my mother to help take care of my brother and sister, and to make sure Mom was holding her own.

After our stepfather left, my mother went to work in a restaurant-bar called the Midway Café located across the street from the Fort

Thomas military base. Over the years, she would find work at several bars. We often lived upstairs or behind a tavern so she wouldn't have to walk too far to go to work or to drink.

She farmed all of us out from time to time to relatives because she couldn't take care of us on her own. Every four or five months, though, she'd find a new place, and often we would go back with her for a while. She did her best to keep us together as a family.

The more she deteriorated, the stronger I tried to become. In effect, I began to assume the role of parent of the family.

"We don't have to live like this," I would say to my mother over and over.

Despite her failings, my mother wanted us to have the best possible education, and she insisted I enroll in Fort Thomas at Highlands High School, which was considered the best in the area. But I felt socially awkward there. Most of my classmates had money, and I didn't. I didn't look or dress like anyone else. A lot of my clothing was tattered and torn. I think I had one pair of jeans for school, two corduroy shirts and a couple of flannel shirts, and that was it.

After a while there, I became a loner with a chip on my shoulder – a lot of chips, to be honest.

I always had the feeling of being kind of the black sheep of our family; some people thought I was trouble even when I did nothing wrong. I was an angry young man. Look at me the wrong way and I'd let you know. Cross me and you got worse. I ended up in quite a few fistfights as a teenager, even though I wasn't a big kid. I was very thin at the time and probably undernourished.

I made the freshman football team but quit after the coach didn't put me into games. I never thought sitting on the bench was appropriate. My attitude was: Either you play me or I'm out of here. I also joined the marching band and learned to play the tuba.

However, I missed a lot of classes in high school because I was taking just about any job I could find. I made a dime here, a nickel there. I gave most of it to Mom, although I put some money aside to make sure she didn't use it for things she didn't need, which primarily was alcohol. I got a job on a farm. I worked on trash pickup. I delivered newspapers. I upholstered furniture.

I worked for quite a while in a bowling alley setting pins. In those days we didn't have automatic pinsetters. I physically set two lanes at a time. It was very hard work. The job could be dangerous, being so close to all those bowling pins flying around.

On one occasion, I looked up the alley and saw a couple of guys who had been drinking beer while bowling. When they took a break, I went to one of them and said, "How you'd like to win?"

The guy said, "What are you talking about?"

"I can fix it so that you win."

He got the joke right away. When they resumed bowling, whenever his ball went down the alley, I secretly would take a pin and throw it in there, and the guy would get a strike every time. I loved doing stuff like that.

The job at the bowling alley also involved sweeping lanes with a large broom, then going back with another broom to oil the lanes once or twice a night. I'd also go to the cashier's area to work on concessions and to rent out shoes.

I always had my school books with me. During the breaks between games, I would try to study.

One day someone told the owner I had stolen money from the cash register, and right away he told me I had to go.

I said, "Why?"

"You took money."

"I didn't take money," I said, but he didn't believe me. I knew, in fact, that one of his relatives had been stealing cash from the register, but I didn't have any proof. The owner repeated that I was fired.

I walked to the second floor to get my school books one last time. While there, I looked out the window and saw a car parked just below. It was a brand-new vehicle owned by the relative I had seen stealing the money. I picked up two bowling balls and dropped them on the car, smashing the front window and doing quite a bit of other damage. The owner called the cops. The only thing that kept me from being sent to a reform school is that my mother's brother-in-law, William Wright, was a captain at the Fort Thomas Police Department. He saved me.

My whole personality was displayed in that one incident. I was never a bad person, but I just didn't take any crap from anybody. I tried to be a hard and honest worker, but don't try to cheat me. Don't mess with me.

***

One day in spring 1955, Grandpa Collins went down along the Ohio River to repair the engine on the Ferry Princess docked at Brent. The 30-foot boat, which transported passengers across the river to Coney Island of Ohio, was a converted World War II landing craft. The boat could transport up to 30 people at a time. I think the toll was 50 cents for a child, $1 for an adult.

Grandpa had soon talked the ferry's owner, John D. Laughead, into giving me a job as an apprentice. "Johnny" Laughead was quite a character. He had started the ferry in 1936 after people kept asking for rides on his rowboat he had docked in Brent. He once told the *Cincinnati Enquirer* that Fort Thomas Army base promised him a draft deferment in World War II if he kept the ferry available in case of enemy invasion. He did – and he was drafted anyway into the Navy, where he served as a radio operator in the South Pacific. After the war, he resumed operations of the Ferry Princess and purchased a second boat, the Ferry Prince, as part of a contract with Coney Island.

Laughead immediately put me to work handling lines and helping to collect tolls. I loved working on the river, loved interacting with passengers and, most of all, loved how the work put distance between me and the troubles back home. Literally and figuratively, working on the Ferry Princess helped to keep my head above water.

John D. Laughead, owner of the Brent Ferry, is seen in September 1976 on the Ferry Prince. (Photo courtesy of the Kenton County Public Library, Covington, Kentucky.)

The only problem was, even after two or three weeks on the job, Laughead still hadn't paid me. He hadn't even mentioned a salary.

When I told my grandmother, she told me to "pay yourself."

"Give yourself 50 cents or a dollar an hour. You're collecting the tolls. Laughead doesn't keep track of them. Just pay yourself," she said.

So, at the end of the day, without telling Laughead, I'd put $5 into my pocket, and that was the end of it. Or so I thought.

One Friday night after the end of the season, Grandpa Collins took me to a German tavern in Newport. He was having a beer. I was drinking Coca-Cola. The bar was full of these German-American men, and Laughead was there, too. One of the men at the bar saw me and said, "How do you like working on the river?" I said, "It's a lot of fun. I really enjoy it."

And then one turned to Laughead and asked how much he was paying me.

"He's an apprentice. He's still learning," he said.

My grandfather said, "What? You didn't pay him?"

And the other men in the bar – all older guys – piped up, telling Laughead to stop being cheap and to pay the kid.

Right then, these men took up a collection to pay me one way or another. The next thing I knew I had 60 bucks in my pocket. Even Laughead threw in some money. He still didn't know I had secretly been paying myself.

Through the summer of the next year, I continued to work for Laughead, including chipping paint and doing other chores to keep the Ferry Princess and the Ferry Prince looking good.

All and all, Laughead was very good to me. He even let me run the boat across the river when heading back from Coney Island with no passengers on board. It was a very easy boat to operate. You just had to keep the bow up in the current because it didn't have a lot of power. Occasionally rain and wind blew down the Ohio River, but if it got bad, we docked the boat until the storm blew over.

The weather was fine one day in late 1956 as we were returning the Ferry Princess across the river to Brent. There were no passengers aboard when the engines suddenly died. The ferry began drifting down the river as we tried to restart the engines. I looked up at one point to see us heading right for the most beautiful boat on the river, the Delta Queen.

2. The Queen

THE Ferry Princess drifted on until, remarkably near Cincinnati, we managed to lay the boat safely alongside the Delta Queen, which by the mid-1950s was one of the last steam-powered ships to operate in the U.S. with a stern-mounted paddlewheel. (In fact, she would be designated a National Historic Landmark in 1989.) I was invited aboard the Queen while its engineers came down to help fix the engines.

How the Delta Queen ended up as a passenger cruise ship on the Ohio, Mississippi, Tennessee and Cumberland rivers is a marvelous sea story of its own. She was constructed in 1926 in Scotland at 285 feet long and 58 feet wide, with a capacity of 176 passengers, then transported in pieces to California where she was reassembled. The Queen had been built for luxury, with hardwood paneling, brass fittings, stained glass windows and a large staircase over which hung a crystal chandelier.

The Delta Queen – and a second ship, the Delta King – spent their early years carrying overnight passengers on the Sacramento River in California. During World War II, the U.S. Navy used the ships to ferry troops in San Francisco and to transport wounded men to hospitals.

In 1946, Tom Greene, owner of Greene Line Steamers in Cincinnati, paid $46,000 for the Delta Queen to add the ship to its family-owned passenger service. The only problem was how to transport it to the Mississippi River. The solution was to brace the ship and box it up in unpainted wood like "a huge piano box" for an ocean voyage, according to a marvelous account of the journey in the 1950 book *The Saga of the Delta Queen,* by Frederick Way Jr. Accompanied by a tugboat, the Queen departed from Antioch, California, on April 18, 1947. It endured a brief grounding on a mudflat before it reached the ocean, where squalls and rolling seas created a perilous trip down the California coast.

A tugboat escorts the Delta Queen east through the Panama Canal on May 11, 1947, toward the Gulf of Mexico and its destination of Cincinnati. (Photo courtesy of the collection of the Public Library of Cincinnati and Hamilton County.)

At 1:30 p.m. Saturday, May 10, under partly cloudy skies but with good visibility, the Delta Queen arrived on the Pacific side of the Panama Canal. A canal pilot, Captain Sorenson, came aboard at 2:30 p.m. to take control of navigation. After a night in Panama, the journey resumed the next morning, entering Miraflores Locks at 7:27

and Pedro Miguel Locks at 8:30. After crossing Gatun Lake, the ship entered Gatun Locks at 2:08 p.m. before proceeding out to the Caribbean Sea at 3:30, soon rolling and pitching on the ocean.

On Monday, May 19, the Delta Queen arrived at the mouth of the Mississippi River, then traveled to Pittsburgh to be overhauled.

Tragically, in 1950, three years after he oversaw the Delta Queen's return to passenger service, Tom Greene died of a heart problem at age 47. It would be up to his widow, Letha Greene, to take on the responsibilities of operating Greene Line Steamers and the Delta Queen.

In fact, when the Princess Ferry drifted alongside the Delta Queen in summer 1956, it was Mrs. Greene who greeted me. She brought me aboard the ship for lunch while members of her crew were fixing the ferry's engines. She told me I was always welcome to come back.

"If you ever get a chance, come visit me. We tie up here in Cincinnati over the winter. Maybe I can find something for you to do," she said.

After the summer, during a break in school, I went down to Newport and over the bridge. I saw the Delta Queen docked and Mrs. Greene right there.

I introduced myself. She said, "Do I know you?"

"Yes, ma'am. This past summer your people helped me a little bit on the river."

"Oh, yes," she said, "Well, come aboard. I'll give you lunch."

The next thing I knew I was wandering over to the Delta Queen on weekends, just hanging out, because I loved to be with those people. They were so nice to me. They gave me work with a paintbrush and other little jobs to do in exchange for lunch.

Eventually, one of the crew members said to Mrs. Greene, "I think we should start paying this kid." She agreed, and she began giving me 50 cents an hour to work on the riverboat.

During the winter I'd even sleep on board when the Delta Queen tied up near Cincinnati for maintenance. Then in April when it sailed down the river for its first trip of the season, I just stayed aboard. No one said anything. I was kind of an apprentice seaman, took coffee to the guys in the wheelhouse, and just helped where I could. Best of all, the Delta Queen crew became like a second family, a group of people happy I was around, and I was happy to work for them, even if it meant missing school. I just went to classes when I felt like it. After I read some books by Mark Twain, that was it. I decided I was another Tom Sawyer playing hooky on a river adventure.

I was having lunch one time when Mrs. Greene sat down with me and asked how I was doing.

After I told her I was doing great, I added, "I'd like to be a boat captain someday."

She said, "Kenny, you're a good worker. If that's your goal, then someday you will find a way to reach it."

In March 1957, I was working on the Delta Queen when we were boarded by the Steamship Authority while the riverboat was being readied for the season. In those days the riverboats were overseen by the authority, which inspected the safety systems and made sure everything was otherwise in order. When someone from the authority spotted this skinny kid who wasn't in school, he asked me my age and requested to see my working papers, which I didn't have.

Mrs. Greene tried to talk her way out of it. She explained I was just a part-timer, but the authorities told her I needed the papers anyway. I wasn't even on the Delta Queen's payroll books. Besides, what was I doing working on a riverboat instead of going to classes?

At one point they were going to call a magistrate and treat me as a kind of juvenile delinquent. Fortunately, a guy from the authority called my grandmother, who verified who I was and explained my mother's financial situation.

"He's not a bad kid," my grandmother said of me. "He just wants to work."

In fact, right after I was sent home, I got hired to serve customers at the Dairy Queen in Fort Thomas. The first day there, the woman who ran the fast-food restaurant said to me, "Now, Ken, if you ever get hungry, if you ever feel like you need something to eat, go ahead and fix yourself something." Then she left. In those days they'd let teenagers run things by themselves.

I was there for three or four days when she came over to me and said, "Ken, you're working pretty well. You're doing a good job. But you've eaten 12 hamburgers in three days. Unfortunately, I have to let you go. You're eating too much." So, she let me go. I guess she learned that you don't tell a teenage boy to go ahead and eat if he's hungry.

Although times were tough at home, it wasn't that bad on the outside. I was fortunate to find two decent young men who looked after me: Bill Thornton and Tom Macht.

Bill's family took me in at various times, gave me his hand-me-down clothes, took me to church, fed me and helped to keep me focused. His mom became like my second mother. Even after I went into the military and then to Panama, they were like an extended family. Bill has since passed away, leaving his wonderful wife, Barbara, five children and 25 grandchildren.

Tom was my buddy, gave me support and provided me transportation to work. In the late 1950s, I got a part-time job sweeping floors at McAlpin's department store in downtown Cincinnati. This provided the opportunity to attend "Bob Braun's Teen Dance Band Radio Show" sponsored by McAlpin's on Saturdays at the store. One of the show's producers asked me to put on some young men's clothes and to model them during the show. In agreeing, I got to keep some of them. Tom, who to this day remains a close friend, often reminds me: "You are the only person I have ever heard who modeled clothing on a radio show."

The spring of 1958 when I was a member of the track team at school, I always carefully hung up my uniform in the basement. I came home once to find that Mom had pulled it off the line and threw it in the corner. When I picked it up, it smelled just like beer.

I went to my Uncle Bill, the police captain, and poured out my frustrations.

I stand with classmates in the back row, center, is this photo from Highlands High School's 1957 yearbook. In the caption I was listed as K. Combs.

"What am I going to do?" I asked him.

He said, "Hang around here much longer, I know what you're going to do. You and your mother are really going to get into it. You're at the point now I worry you could get physical with her."

Things weren't any better at school. I was sitting in the library when a teacher who had always been a bit nasty said to me, "Kenneth, how many days a week are you going to wear that flannel shirt?"

I reacted by picking up my school books and angrily throwing them in the corner.

"I'm leaving this friggin' place. I'm getting out of here," I said.

The teacher tried to calm me down.

"What are you going to do?" she said.

I looked out the window and – swear to God – passing by the school was a van that had "U.S. Navy" printed on the side. I looked back at the teacher and said, "I'm going in the Navy." I walked out the door, got on a bus and went over to Cincinnati and, yes, enlisted in the Navy.

When I came home early, my mother asked, "Why aren't you in school?"

"I quit," I said. "I'm going in the Navy."

"Is that a fact?" she said.

She didn't try to talk me out of it. She actually thought it was a good idea, even if it meant dropping out of school.

"It's about time you went somewhere," she said. "You're getting to be a real pain in the neck."

"That's all right. I'll be gone in a few days."

I think I realized, too, I needed to get out of Dodge. I still had my temper, and I knew it could only mean more trouble for me if I stayed. There was nothing I could do to save my brother, sister and mother from the situation we were living in, and I knew I could no longer lean on my grandparents to take care of me.

Shortly after that, I had my physical and did paperwork at the Navy induction center in Fort Thomas. There was some confusion at the time because I had been going by the name Kenneth Combs, and I couldn't find my birth certificate.

"I know the Navy induction petty officer," my mother told me. She saw him at the bar all the time.

She said, "Let me talk to him about your birth certificate." She came back and told me the petty officer said the Navy agreed to take me without one. But I would need to enlist under my real name, Kenneth Paul Puckett.

At the time we knew a local guy, Sam Rayburn, who did a little of everything. He was a constable; he also had an insurance business, a funeral home and a barbershop. I think he may even have run the fire department sometimes. When he found out I was leaving for the Navy, Sam said to me, "You got to come to the barbershop and get a haircut. I cut it when you were a kid, and I'm going to cut it now." When he was done, I don't think I could have backed out of the Navy, because I was just about bald. He pretty much took every bit of hair right off.

Before I left, I visited my grandparents. I sat on the front stoop with Grandpa Collins eating watermelon while he had a beer and talked about the Navy.

Soon, I noticed a few tears in his eyes.

"Grandpa, what are you crying about?"

He pulled up his sleeve and showed me some of his tattoos, then pulled up a pants leg and showed me more.

"You can go in the Navy, but you do not get tattoos. It's the worst thing that can happen. You promise me, no tattoos."

"Okay, Grandpa, no tattoos."

I guess it was his way of telling me not to do something that I would spend a lifetime regretting.

On April 18, 1958, with a 10th-grade education, a very short haircut and no birth certificate, I was sworn into the Navy and shipped up to the Naval Training Center at Great Lakes, Illinois, for basic training.

3. The Navy

WHEN I was growing up, I loved music. I used to have the radio on all the time. Music was a way I tried to drown out all the turmoil in my life. I think that's why I started playing tuba and joined the marching band in high school. When I got to the naval boot camp, I volunteered to play tuba in the recruit musical band. The Navy used the band to identify sailors to train at its music school. Even though I wasn't good enough to get selected for that, it was worth being in the band, for no other reason that doing so got me exempt from washing dishes and other kitchen duties.

Very quickly, I fell in love with Navy life. Beginning with boot camp, I settled right down. It so perfectly suited me. It gave me three meals a day, clothing, guidelines, rules, regulations, and I fit right in. It was where I belonged. My temperament changed overnight. The Navy was my salvation.

When I finished recruit training in July 1958, I volunteered and was accepted at the Navy's submarine school in New London, Connecticut. I wasn't there long when a crisis broke out in the Middle East; Lebanese President Camille Chamoun asked for U.S. military intervention to protect his country against an internal uprising as well as threats from Egypt and Syria. The Naval Submarine Base grabbed a bunch of us out of class and assigned us to help get operational a couple of submarines for deployment to the Mediterranean. The plan was for most of the students to eventually return to class or, in some cases, get assigned to a sub without completing basic school.

That's me with a big grin in a photo taken by the U.S. Navy in 1958 during boot camp at the Navy's training center in Great Lakes, Illinois.

Over the next few weeks, I would be assigned to two submarines, including the USS Sea Robin (SS-407), a vessel named after a bottom-dwelling fish with spiny fins and armor plating. The Sea Robin was a 312-foot-long diesel-electric sub built during World War II for a crew of 10 officers and 70 enlisted men.

One of my assignments aboard was to maintain a notebook for the captain. How I got the job, I don't know because I couldn't write very well, and my penmanship was even worse. Even my printing was so bad the captain warned me I better shape up.

"If you're going to continue doing this for me, you better learn to write right. If you don't, you're not only going to be off this boat, you're going to be out of submarine service," he said.

Intent on self-improvement, I turned to a bulletin board on the submarine with 3-by-5 cards from young women all over the United States and Canada who wanted to correspond with a sailor. I thought if I wrote to one, it would please her while it would also give me the practice to better my writing. I responded to one of the cards with a card of my own. Two weeks later, I got a letter back from this young lady from Connecticut. And with it, she sent me a box of cookies. I thought, boy, this is even better than I thought.

So, I took down a card from another young woman. And another. I ended up responding to cards from four women. Except for changing her name and address, I just copied word for word the first card I sent, always ending it with, "P.S. If you get a chance, come visit my ship." Sure enough, I got letters with photos of the women, as well as more cookies. I thought I was a genius.

Around September, we returned to shore after a weeklong exercise. I was in the conning tower on top relaying messages from the captain to the control room when I looked down at the dock and, without thinking, I blurted out a few four-letter superlatives.

"What did you say, Puckett?" the captain asked.

I had violated one unwritten rule sailors learned in the Navy at that time: The only one allowed to curse in the presence of the captain was the chief petty officer. But I had bigger things on my mind.

"Sir," I said, "you can take me and put me in the torpedo tube and fire it, because I am in trouble."

"Why is that?"

"Sir, there are three young ladies standing over there," I said, pointing toward the dock. "They all came to see me."

By the time we pulled into the dock, the women had figured out they were all there to see the same sailor, and two of them were very angry about it. Some of the crew tried to find me, but I had already inched my skinny frame behind the previously mentioned torpedo tubes and remained hidden there until the women departed, one of them on the arm of another sailor.

In 1958, the United States was just beginning to develop nuclear submarines. The Sea Robin, like most subs at the time, used old-fashioned electric engines that operated on diesel fuel. The engines continued to feed off diesel so long as it kept its snorkel above the surface to draw in air and to exhaust it.

I was sleeping in my bunk when an order came to dive below snorkel depth. The crew closed the snorkel, and the engine room transferred power over to batteries. This brief transfer process drew a sudden partial vacuum in the boat. I quickly woke up with a sharp pain in my ears. It was not unlike the effect airplane passengers feel in their ears when the pressure changes. The force on a submarine, though, was so strong it could rupture eardrums if the sailor wasn't used to it. Submariners were taught how to hold their nose and blow to equalize the pressure. Even so, this effect probably stretched many eardrums over time. I'm sure there wasn't a submariner from World War II who didn't have permanent ear problems because of it.

After this incident aboard the Sea Robin, I started getting headaches, and I soon ended up with an ear infection requiring a visit to Saint Albans Naval Hospital in Long Island, New York. After treatment, I was told it could take months before my ears were well enough to resume submarine duty. Meanwhile, I failed a submarine aptitude test. Put it all together, and I was disqualified for submarine service and on my way in November 1958 to an assignment aboard the aircraft carrier USS Valley Forge (CVS 45). I was so disappointed. I wanted to remain assigned to a submarine, if for no other reason than the fact its sailors got bonus pay of around $50 a month.

It would be another 30 years, working on the Panama Canal, before I would find myself again on a Navy submarine.

The USS Valley Forge was an 888-foot-long ship built during World War II and named after General George Washington's military encampment. Almost like a small city, the carrier had a crew of about 260 officers and 2,300 seamen, in addition to pilots and crew for more than 100 aircraft.

As with other World War II-era aircraft carriers, it had what was called an "open flight deck." The carriers today have hurricane bows, enclosed all the way up to the flight deck to protect against high waves, but we didn't have that then.

When I came aboard the Valley Forge, it was part of an anti-submarine attack carrier group with fixed-wing planes aboard that dropped sonar sensors to detect the movements of Soviet submarines in the area. The Valley Forge sailed as part of the Alpha Group, which included a couple of submarines and four or five Navy destroyers.

My initial assignment was chipping paint and other mundane tasks. After a few weeks, one of the chief petty officers moved me to the navigation department on the bridge. Why he decided to do this, I'm still not sure. Perhaps he saw some potential in me, including a willingness to volunteer for any open assignment – a trait that I would embrace throughout my military career. In the navigation department, I was given the job of winding the ship's clocks – 140 or so of them. It was a favorite job of mine, as I got to be familiar with almost every nook and cranny on the aircraft carrier.

I strike a pose while standing guard duty during Navy recruit training in May 1958.

I also became a helmsman trainee, working on the bridge and learning how to steer the ship. On an aircraft carrier in those days, the Navy always had 25 to 30 sailors qualified to steer the ship under normal conditions. The carriers didn't have automatic pilots back then; there was a helmsman at the wheel at all times. The navigation department had two officers, two chiefs and a bunch of enlisted seamen. The carrier also had a helmsman stationed in the aft steering room, which is an emergency station in the back of the ship.

In early January 1959, I was on duty on the bridge when the ship was being tossed by a winter storm off Cape Hatteras, North Carolina. It was rough. The ship was rolling like you wouldn't believe due to 25-to 30-foot seas, and winds were blowing over gale force at 65 to 75 miles an hour. The visibility was maybe six to eight miles. It was so bad the crew tied down all the planes, and other ships in our flotilla were told to disperse so we wouldn't accidentally collide with each other.

During the storm, you could hear the Valley Forge moan and groan. Even in good weather, at night you heard a lot of creaking. The metal on older ships typically becomes more flexible as they age, and the metal on this one was no exception.

I was up on the bridge when, suddenly out of the fog and mist, we spotted a merchant ship bearing down on us about eight miles off our port side. We had three radar systems, yet somehow the radars didn't pick up this threat coming straight at us.

"Hard right rudder. All ahead full on the port engine," Captain William Morgan McCormick ordered.

With the starboard engine slowing, the ship quickly turned abeam to the seas, and the ship began rolling 25 to 30 degrees. That sudden turn made the carrier vulnerable to those churning seas. As the ship rolled, a huge wave came underneath that open flight deck and caved in the forward end. Several planes in the hangar deck broke loose and sustained serious damage. I heard later that we lost a few planes over the side, but I'm not sure we did. There were no deaths, but quite a few sailors got banged up pretty good.

The good news is we missed colliding with the commercial ship. Captain McCormick's maneuver saved the Valley Forge from catastrophic damage. But with a caved-in flight deck, we had to head for Norfolk, Virginia. We spent several weeks there unloading all our bombs and rockets, as well as a lot of jet fuel, before we headed for the naval shipyard in New York City for three months of repairs to the flight deck. To repair the Valley Forge, the Navy shipyard cut the forward section off our sister ship, the USS Franklin, that had been mothballed in New Jersey. It used that flight deck section to replace the damaged section of the Valley Forge.

The aircraft carrier USS Valley Forge (CVS-45) is missing part of its port side after it was torn away when heavy seas struck the ship in January 1959 when I was aboard. (U.S. Navy photo, from the collections of the Naval Historical Center.)

***

I continued my work on the bridge. One morning around 6 o'clock, the chief petty officer turned to me and asked if I knew how to make a pot of coffee for the bridge crew.

"Yes, sir."

The truth was, I never had made coffee on the Valley Forge. But my grandfather told me one time, "If you're going to be successful in the military, always volunteer, even for the dirty jobs. Because they'll learn they can count on you and then they'll give you the good jobs."

I headed to the back of the conning tower where a 40-cup coffee urn stood duty. I saw where I needed to put in the water, and I noted how much coffee to use. Then I looked inside and saw the pot was scuzzy – greasy and black with coffee stains and oils and looking generally unhealthy. I went to a deep sink and proceeded to scrub that pot until it was just as shiny on the inside as it was on the outside. Only then did I make an urn of coffee, carefully following directions to get all the right measurements.

I finished the coffee and headed for breakfast about 7 below deck in the mess hall. I returned a while later to the navigation bridge, where I noticed this line of men waiting to use the toilets.

The chief immediately walked over to me.

"Did you make this coffee?"

"I did, sir," I said proudly.

"You little SOB," he shouted. "I'm going to whip you within one inch of your life."

I wondered if I made the coffee too strong.

"What's wrong, chief?" I asked. "I made it according to the instructions."

"Did you really? Let me show you something." He led me to the coffee urn.

I peered inside at the bottom, where I spotted a small object that I knew didn't belong in a coffee pot. It was a half-pound bar of Navy lye soap. I had accidentally left it there during my diligent cleaning.

Men on the bridge were now in two lines going into the "head" – the Navy term for its toilet. (The Army uses the word "latrine.") My coffee was going through those men like a freight train. About 15 to 20 guys were totally wiped out.

"You're off the bridge," the chief barked at me, "and I'm confining you to quarters."

He wasn't done. "And when you're down there," he added, "you will clean the toilets and clean the crew quarters. And when you're not doing that, you'll be working as a mess cook in the galley."

As I walked a lonely path back to my quarters, I knew any hopes for a stellar career in the Navy had ended. I was back in the second division, assigned to cleaning duties, which I knew was about the hardest job on the ship. The Navy puts a premium on keeping its ships super-clean. After all, it didn't want anyone to get sick.

About a month into my new assignment, I was told one day to get ready for a locker inspection. I wasn't being singled out. The officers would come down periodically to the crew quarters and order sailors to open their lockers. Almost never would they find a perfect locker – one where everything was folded properly, clean and well-ordered.

I was not looking forward to the inspection. My locker was a mess. It was atrocious, and I was already in trouble for the soap incident. I had no time to properly clean my locker. But I came up with a brilliant plan. A good pal and fellow sailor named Mackelwitz had shared his locker combination with me, so I knew he had the neatest locker I'd ever seen. He wasn't due for inspection, so I decided to quickly switch our locks and tags before the officers arrived.

A lieutenant soon ordered me to open what I'd led him to believe was my locker. He couldn't believe it. He was beside himself.

"Let me tell you something, Seaman Puckett. This is unbelievable. I've never seen a locker this neat before," he said.

He thought a sailor with a locker that neat and orderly deserved a better assignment than cleaning toilets. He turned to the chief who accompanied him.

"Here's the next lineman for the captain's gig," he said.

A "captain's gig" in the Navy is a small, supplemental landing craft used to transport the ship's captain to shore when the ship is too big to come into a port. Working on the Valley Forge captain's gig was a coveted job for the four-man crew. When we were at sea, all we had to do was keep that gig spit-polished and clean. We didn't have to stand any watches or do anything else.

***

In January 1960, the Valley Forge anchored about eight miles off-shore at Hamilton, Bermuda, while those of us in charge of the gig took Captain McCormick to the island for official calls and to visit a couple of British navy clubs. We pulled into the port, and the captain went ashore. Not long afterward, the gig coxswain, who was a second-class petty officer; the engineer; and the leading handler all headed to a nearby restaurant. They said they would be back long before the captain was due to return. Because I was the junior line handler, I was told to stay behind to look after the gig.

"We'll bring you back something to eat," the gig coxswain added.

They hadn't been gone a half an hour when back came Captain McCormick. He informed me he had spilled some wine on his white uniform and needed to immediately return to the aircraft carrier to change.

"Where's the rest of the crew?" he asked, looking around.

I said that they had gone to get something to eat and that I would fetch them.

"No, you don't. I don't have time for that," he said. "Can you run the boat?"

"Yes, sir. I ran a boat when I was on the Ohio River, and I've watched them run this boat," I said.

"Then get the engine going. We're heading back to the ship."

He helped me to throw the lines off, and away we went. Before long, we were back alongside the Valley Forge, where a couple of sailors jumped aboard and helped to moor the gig alongside the gangway. A couple of other sailors took the captain back to port in Bermuda. Another launch then left to pick up the three guys from the gig crew.

The others in the gig crew were furious at me for not waiting, even though it wasn't my fault.

Several days later, the first lieutenant ordered all four of us to attend a disciplinary hearing known as a "captain's mast." It was a nonjudicial proceeding, not a court-martial. Still, I worried we would all face severe punishments for not properly manning the gig.

Captain McCormick went right down the line of the four of us, one by one busting the three others to lower ranks and removing them from their assignment to his gig. When he got to me, he turned to the first lieutenant and said I didn't deserve to be there because I hadn't abandoned my post. What's more, the captain said, he was putting me in charge of the gig. When the lieutenant reminded McCormick he couldn't do that because I was only a seaman apprentice, the captain ordered him to make me a seaman.

What's more, the captain said, he was putting me in for third-class petty officer in the quartermaster rating pending completion of a required exam. While I would be studying for that, I would also have to work to master such things as signaling, navigation and Morse Code.

In March 1960, after reviewing the examination study materials, I took the fleetwide exam containing 150 multiple choice questions. I immediately left on leave to Kentucky without thinking I had much chance of passing, let alone get the promotion. I guessed there were about 1,700 experienced seamen in the Atlantic Fleet at the time who were more qualified and prepared than me.

I was home visiting my grandmother when I received a long-distance call. It was from the chief petty officer on the Valley Forge with the news that not only had I passed the text, but I would be immediately promoted to third-class petty officer. Apparently, my test score was high enough that it made up for other factors, such as my inexperience and the short time I had been in the Navy. I have no idea how I passed the exam. To this day I believe it to be a miracle that I made third-class petty officer.

When I got back to the Valley Forge, it seemed like everybody was looking at this 19-year-old third-class petty officer and wondering: How the heck did he get that?

***

With my sudden promotion, it was time for me to leave the Valley Forge. The Navy didn't want to have me supervising sailors who up until then had been working with me on an equal status.

In June 1960, I was transferred to the U.S.S. Thomas J. Gary (DER 326), a destroyer escort stationed at the Navy base in Newport, Rhode Island. The Gary was assigned to "radar picket" duty in the North Atlantic. The ship used its radars and other electronic equipment to detect Russian aircraft flying south of Greenland and Russian submarines trying to sneak in. We were there looking for them, and they were there looking for us.

Not long after I arrived, I went up the bridge and introduced myself to the chief petty officer.

"OK, Puckett, you're a third-class petty officer. You take the first watch," he said.

"Where do I take it?" I said flippantly, instantly regretting having done so.

While the chief petty officer pondered my stunning insubordination, I quickly explained that I never actually worked on the bridge except for winding clocks, steering the ship, making coffee and bringing up smoke flares. I told him my last assignment aboard the carrier was as captain's gig coxswain.

"Can you keep a quartermaster's watch?" he asked.

"No"

"Can you signal?" he asked.

"No."

"Can you use navigation equipment?"

"No," I said. "I never did the practical factors checklist. All I did was take the exam and pass it."

Now, this part gets a little technical, but bear with me a little bit.

The "practical factors checklist" is a system Navy sailors go through that requires them to show that they can perform a series of given skill tasks for their rating. After they complete the checklist, they are then recommended to take the examination in that respective petty officer rating. I was now a third-class petty officer who had never completed the practical factors checklist for third-class petty officer in the quartermaster rating.

The chief petty officer wanted to remove my stripe right there. He ordered me off the bridge and then took the problem to the captain. Fortunately, the captain decided it wasn't my fault I was promoted without the practical training. He decided to give me three months to learn all the things on the checklist – and he also ordered me to remain on the ship until I had completed each of them, or I could give up the promotion.

For the next 97 days, the chief himself took me under his wing and trained me on the practical factors on the checklist. Until I passed those practical factors and he knew he could trust me with standing a navigational watch on the bridge, I could not go ashore.

By the end, I was qualified, and the chief assigned me to a navigation watch.

The work on that checklist also more than qualified me for the next higher rating. So, in June 1961, I became eligible for promotion to second-class petty officer-quartermaster. I was recommended by the chief, passed the next advanced practical factors checklist, and passed the written exam with a 92 percent mark. I was then promoted and designated as one of the ship's enlisted navigators.

***

When I wasn't at sea, I lived in downtown Newport, Rhode Island, in an apartment I shared with a friend. I bought a late-model, beautiful blue pickup truck. Grandpa Collins had told me, "If you want to make friends, get a pickup truck. People will always be friendly because somebody will always want to borrow your pickup." To a young man in search of female companionship, that sounded like a good plan.

Sure enough, I didn't have that truck three days when this young woman down the hallway in the apartment building came over looking to use the truck. We soon began dating, and she made a kind offer to look after my vehicle when I was at sea. "I'll drive you back to the ship and bring the truck back and park it for you. I'll even help you wash it," she said. I thought: Wow, Grandpa, you really were right.

One morning, the ship was heading out to sea, and I wanted to be there in plenty of time before its 8 o'clock departure. My girlfriend got up early to drop me off around 6. After she drove away, I noticed I forgot my kit pack with underwear, toiletries and shaving kit. I quickly headed back down the gangway and grabbed a taxi cab to the apartment, which was only a mile or two away.

I had the taxi wait outside while I got my kit. I glanced over and saw my pickup truck was back in its parking spot. I retrieved my kit and was walking out of the building when I saw the truck take off out of the lot. I could see my girlfriend in the driver's seat. Next to her was another sailor I didn't recognize.

"Follow that truck!" I said to the cab driver, like I was some detective in an old movie.

Off we went in this pursuit through the streets. I don't know if they saw us or not. But this chase continued until, finally, I gave up. It was 7:45 a.m. and I needed to get back to the ship by 8 or risk court-martial for missing departure. As it was, they had already pulled up lines when I jumped aboard.

When I got to the bridge, the captain was already there. He must have seen me running down the pier. But he never said a word about it.

We were out to sea about a week when I was ordered with several other sailors to appear before a captain's disciplinary proceeding. I faced three charges brought by a first lieutenant, whom I knew disliked me. He charged me with being absent without leave (AWOL), absent over liberty, and missing movement – all related to that hurried arrival after chasing my pickup. I knew I wasn't AWOL or absent without liberty because I got there before the ship sailed. I guess I "missed movement" because the lines were in, which meant technically the ship was underway.

The captain quickly dismissed the first two charges. I guess he decided the third was such a minor violation that he declined to reduce my rank. Instead, he restricted me to 30 days on the ship when we got back to port. I was relieved that I didn't lose my stripes.

But before he dismissed me, the captain said, "I want you to tell me the story as to why this all happened."

I gave him the whole story of how I saw my girlfriend giving another sailor a ride in my pickup truck while she thought I was safely aboard the ship.

"Unfortunately, sir, I never did find out who he was," I said.

The captain smiled. "I never heard that story before. We hear a lot of stories up here, but that's a good one."

"It's the truth, sir."

"Okay. If you don't have any further incident for 30 days, this whole thing will be expunged from your record."

"Thank you very much, Captain."

"Okay, dismissed. Next."

As I was leaving the captain turned to a young petty officer who had missed the ship entirely the same day I barely made it aboard.

"Okay, what's your explanation?" the captain asked the petty officer.

"Sir," the sailor said, "I was the guy in his pickup."

The captain just broke up laughing.

"Maybe you two made up this one together, but it is the best story I ever heard."

The captain gave the other petty officer 30 days of confinement, too.

***

I had done well for myself in the Navy. But by summer 1962, I was ready to move on. During my time in the service, I received my high school equivalency diploma. I was eager to get a college education and get into teaching. I planned to enroll at the University of Kentucky and pay for the tuition using "orphan's benefits" available to children of soldiers killed in the line of duty in World War II.

That July, after four years and three months of military service, I was honorably discharged from the Navy. After returning home, I headed for the Veterans Administration office to fill out the necessary paperwork to qualify for my tuition benefits.

An employee at the VA looked through records for Army Sgt. Nute Puckett. The records listed my brother, Ron, as a survivor.

But then the VA guy dropped a bombshell that changed my life: "We don't show any record that Nute Puckett had a son named Kenneth," he said.

4. George Archey

THE Veterans Administration had to be mistaken. That was my first reaction to being told it had no records showing Nute Puckett was my father. I was sure it was an error caused by me being enrolled in school as Kenneth Combs. The VA told me to bring it a copy of my birth certificate if I wanted to prove Nute Puckett was my father.

I immediately went home and asked my mother to get me a copy, but she said she couldn't do that, and she refused to explain why.

Then I went to various aunts and uncles, and none of them could shed any light on my missing birth certificate. I was sure Grandpa and Grandma Collins would have helped me sort all this out, but he died in 1959 and she died in 1961.

I kept asking and asking, and finally a great-aunt – the family gossip – sat down and told me the truth: Nute Puckett, she said, was not my biological father. I was stunned into silence as my aunt continued a story that began more than two decades earlier.

When my mother was 18, she met an engineering contractor working on a highway near her home. His name was George Archey. He was 29 years old, a native Kentuckian and apparently a pretty good talker. They dated for a while and, eventually, he proposed to my mother and gave her an engagement ring. (My aunt showed me several photos of them together.)

In summer 1940, before they were married, my mother became pregnant with me, and George Archey was the father. A pregnant woman who wasn't married was scandalous in our rural community. But it got even worse for my mother. Archey had failed to tell her he couldn't marry her because he had a wife since 1933, they had two young sons, and his wife was pregnant with their third child.

I later found out this was not the first time George Archey had been in trouble since he got married. A story published November 2, 1934, in the *Cincinnati Enquirer* described how he suffered a cut under his left eye a couple of days earlier during what police described as a Halloween "rumpus" in Covington, Kentucky.

After learning about my mother's pregnancy, there were negotiations. Archey's wife, Mayble, offered to take me and to raise me with her boys. But my grandmother said, "Nobody's taking my first grandson." Poor though she was, she had her pride. Archey would eventually move his family to Tennessee and apparently make no effort to contact me over the years.

A short time after I was born in 1941, Mom met young Nute Puckett and married him and gave birth to his son, Ron, my half-brother. Nute never adopted me.

Whether I knew it or not, I had grown up as a "disgrace to the family," as a cousin later described it to me. To try to protect me, my mother and others did all they could to hide the truth, even from me. It might have remained hidden if Nute Puckett hadn't died in World War II and I hadn't sought out orphan's benefits two decades later.

For the first time, a lot of things made sense about my childhood, including the lack of contact with the Puckett family. So many people had treated me like the black sheep of the family. As my aunt told me, "We never thought you'd amount to anything."

After I learned about George Archey, I went through a very traumatic time emotionally. I felt betrayed, an outcast in my own family. I wandered around for a while in a bit of depression.

Fortunately, I had friends in Kentucky who consoled me and pointed out that I should be proud of my military service and that I should return to that because that's where I was truly at home.

In September 1962, three months after I left the Navy, I went back to the recruiting office and re-enlisted. I continued to call myself Kenneth Paul Puckett, even though I now knew it legally wasn't my name.

I also made a vow to myself: I didn't know where George Archey was living, or even if he was still alive, but I wanted to meet him and to hear his side of the story.

***

When I re-enlisted, I kept my second-class petty officer rating. I also got to choose my next assignment. I requested to serve aboard an aircraft carrier in the Pacific.

I used my re-enlistment bonus to purchase a Chevy convertible. I then drove it to the West Coast, and the Navy had it shipped to me in Honolulu.

On the airplane ride to Hawaii, I met a Navy petty officer who worked in personnel. By the time the flight ended, he had persuaded me to switch my assignment to Armed Forces Police in Honolulu.

"When you are on shore patrol working, you work with the Honolulu Police Department," he said. "You also get an extra $16 a day. And you get police training, so when you get out of the military, you can be a policeman if you want."

That sounded like a smart career move. As a single 21-year-old, I also thought a posting to Hawaii would be a great way to meet attractive female tourists.

I soon reported to duty with Armed Forces Police. The job was fine. I enjoyed it. However, after three months, I felt the lure of sea duty. I decided to switch back to my initial assignment on an aircraft carrier. However, a Navy official informed me, "Sorry, you lost that choice when you joined Armed Forces Police."

Meanwhile, I had been attending dances in Honolulu. There I met Shirley Lewis, a young woman from Canada who worked for

Canadian International Provincial Oil in Honolulu. We kept in touch and, after a whirlwind romance, we were married February 5, 1963, in Hawaii.

I don't think Shirley had a really good idea what she was getting into by marrying an ambitious young Navy guy. In our first year of marriage, I was out to sea 265 days. I didn't really make any adjustment to marriage that normal people make, nor did the military care if I did. The officers used to tell us, "I didn't issue you a bride. So, don't tell me if you got a problem at home." The Navy's attitude was that families were secondary. I sent my paychecks home, but Shirley mostly had to fend for herself, as all the Navy wives did in those days. They had very few support systems.

***

After I left Armed Forces Police, I was assigned to another destroyer escort: the USS Savage (DER-386). Much of my time was now spent on patrols looking for Soviet aircraft in the Bering Sea off the coast of Alaska. It was excellent training, but it was the worst duty in the world. It was an old ship. Living conditions aboard were terrible, and the fresh water system didn't work well. I felt miserable.

It didn't make things any easier when a new chief petty officer came aboard. He decided he needed to get us in better shape as sailors. He had us up in the morning to exercise, regardless of what time we stood watch, and he even put us on a weight machine. It got to the point that we were all fed up with it, but there wasn't anything we could do but follow orders.

I did think of a way to distract him – and get even. When he wasn't looking, I would sneak into his room, pick up his Navy belt, and snip a quarter inch off one end. The next week, I'd go back and take off another quarter inch. I just kept shortening the belt until he almost couldn't get it around his waist.

"Gee," I said to him, "Chief, are you gaining weight?"

He looked at me puzzled. "On my scale, it's fine," he said.

"I don't know," I said. "It sure looks to me like you're gaining weight."

It was a crazy stunt, but that was how we coped aboard Navy ships in that era. Remember, this was the time before the internet, satellite TV, video games and DVD players. We didn't have much entertainment, except to mess with each other.

Another time on the Savage, this same petty officer drove us crazy by hoarding books donated to sailors. We looked forward to these books that the Red Cross and USO would periodically ship to us in boxes, with maybe 40 different titles at one time.

We were thrilled one day when a shipment of books came aboard. But when we asked the chief if it was okay if we handed out the copies, he said, "Nope. I'll read a book first before l pass it out to the crew." Why he did this, I don't know. But it infuriated us.

About two weeks before I was due to leave the ship, I entered his room while he was on shore leave. I opened every one of those boxes and took out all the books. Then with a safety razor, I cut out the last three pages in each book, carefully placing them into separate envelopes with the book titles on each envelope. I took those envelopes with me when I was transferred to another ship.

About three days after I left, the chief got almost all of the way through a book when he discovered the last three pages were missing. He then found that the last three pages were missing in all the books he hoarded.

Periodically I would mail a couple of envelopes with the missing pages back to him. A crew member I met later said the chief petty officer almost went crazy over the incident. He never did learn I was the guy who cut out those pages.

***

Not long after I was married, I was temporarily transferred to another destroyer, the USS Fletcher (DD-445), to supplement the crew as it went from Pearl Harbor, Hawaii, across the Pacific through the Panama Canal to the East Coast. The Fletcher was first in a class of destroyers that served exceptionally well in the Pacific during World War II. By the mid-1960s, although it was an old ship, it remained in very good shape. (The Fletcher was among the ships assigned to the recovery area in the Atlantic when U.S. astronaut Gordon Cooper splashed down in a Mercury space capsule.)

This was my first visit to Panama and my first transit of the canal, and I watched everything intently. I was on the bridge when we arrived in the Bay of Panama. We slowed as someone announced, "We're going to pick up a pilot." Soon a gentleman appeared on the bridge, wearing a white seersucker suit and a light seersucker hat. The captain offered the man a chair and asked if he wanted breakfast. While the pilot waited for the meal, the captain went and person-ally got him a cup of coffee. I was impressed. Usually on a ship, it's the vessel's captain who is treated with such deference.

I was also surprised how the pilot took over operational control, his navigational orders superseding even those of a Navy captain. I'd also never seen that before.

It was springtime with beautiful weather – a nice easy transit. The pilot and a second one who came aboard were very professional in giving directions to ensure there was no damage going through the locks. I remember that the ship had priority, too. A lot of ships were required to get in line and wait a couple of days before they got the opportunity to go through the Panama Canal. But in those days, the U.S. military had a lot of clout. It could cut in line.

***

By the mid-1960s, I was back aboard the Savage and quickly mov-ing up in the ranks. I had been promoted from second-class petty officer to first-class petty officer. With that last promotion, I was transferred to the USS Fletcher, of all ships. The Fletcher was back in

Pearl Harbor as the flagship of Destroyer Squadron 25. I was assigned as the senior quartermaster responsible for monitoring the navigation reports from the other ships in the squadron.

One day I was ashore eating in a cafeteria at Pearl Harbor when I began chatting with a petty officer who was the captain of a Navy harbor tugboat. He explained that the Navy had large tugs that handled ships and submarines that came into the base at Pearl Harbor. He gave me a tour of his tugboat and talked a lot about it. I thought it was a neat job and decided that, when I became a chief petty officer, I would come back and be captain of a tugboat.

After that, whenever the Fletcher came in after maneuvers, I'd go over to the tug and put in some time.

***

In October 1963, my wife gave birth to our daughter, Karen, at Tripler Army Medical Center in Honolulu. I was fortunate to be in port at the time. But having a young child at home didn't transform me into the husband I should have been. I was eager to get back at sea and pursue my career. Even with a child, I put the military first, always. A family was secondary for me. I was immature in that sense. When I was home, I had the habit of most professional military men of communicating with my wife as if she were in the military, too, and therefore had to take orders from me. Once, when Shirley and I had a disagreement, she turned to me and said, "Don't yell at me like I'm one of your seamen."

In April 1965, our second child, Kenneth Thornton Puckett, was born. Tragically he died shortly after birth after suffering a seizure. We buried him at the U.S. Army Schofield Post Barracks Cemetery in Oahu. We were heartbroken. But as before, I was soon back at sea. Not even the death of my son could change my view that the Navy was my top priority.

***

As I mentioned, being aboard a Navy ship in those days was nothing like it is today. My grandson recently spent time aboard a carrier, where he had a nice berthing area, TV with multiple channels, and movie theaters. He could take university classes onboard. He could visit the ship's canteens for sodas and ice cream. We never had any of that in the 1960s, even on the big ships. We had books, and that was about it officially to keep our minds busy during time off.

But I had my own ways to keep things interesting after I became a first-class petty officer and had a navigation department under me. We would be out on the ocean, in the middle of a voyage, and I'd make sure a sailor who was new to sea duty saw me coming down the open deck while I was reading a letter.

Invariably, he would ask, "Did you get mail?"

"Yeah, I got mail."

"Where did you get that?"

I said, "The mail buoy." Then I'd explain that the post office had buoys strategically located throughout the ocean. The post office would fly a seaplane out to a predetermined position. It then would hang a bag on the mail buoy, and we grabbed it as we went by.

"The problem is," I continued, "we don't have enough personnel onboard to be lookouts for those mail buoys. We always need volunteers to go to the bridge, get a pair of binoculars and look for those mail buoys."

The sailor would happily volunteer and go up to the bridge and watch for the mail buoy until he figured out on his own – or someone told him – that I was pulling his leg.

Years later, when I was in the Army as captain of a sea-going tug, I used to get all the mail, go through it and sort it out for each of the departments. I'd also check out the return addresses. It was a way for me to get to know my crew of about 40 men, including where they were from.

I was up on the bridge one time, standing next to this young helmsman who was diligently steering the ship.

"It wasn't like this in Peoria, Illinois," I said casually.

He asked, "You're from Peoria, Captain?"

"Yeah, I'm from Peoria, John. Are you, too?"

"Yes."

"Well, isn't that something? We probably know a lot of the same people in Peoria. I have a young girlfriend up there – her name is Cathy Jones, and she lives on 227 9th Street."

Of course, I didn't know Cathy Jones. I figured out from the return address of his mail that it was his girlfriend, but he didn't know that. Suddenly there I am, the captain, and I just told him we shared the same girlfriend. Before he could say anything, I just walked off knowing he couldn't leave the wheel. He had another two hours of watch.

The senior sergeant in charge of bridge watches came over to me a little while later with a puzzled look.

"What did you say to John up there on the bridge? He's upset, and he's looking all over for you."

"Tell him I'm busy."

I let this poor kid stew for about two days before I let him in on the joke. I guess it was an understandable bit of the devil coming out amid boredom at sea, although a relative later told me, "It's a wonder somebody didn't throw you overboard."

***

In January 1965, I was being considered by the Navy for promotion to commissioned officer. However, I only had a GED high school diploma – and that concerned my detailer at the Navy in Washington.

"The GED isn't good enough," he told me. "You have no college at all."

"But I've got all these technical courses," I said.

"It doesn't matter. If we're going to make you an officer, you need to have a more formal education."

Soon I was transferred to the Navy Leadership and Instructor School in San Diego. In the spring of 1965, a month after I completed the training, I was transferred to the U.S. Naval Reserve and Recruiting Center in Lima, Ohio, and became a Navy recruiter and navigation instructor. While there I also began taking classes at a local college. Once I completed additional college courses, I was told, I would be eligible to go to Officer Candidate School, a real honor for an enlisted sailor.

At the same time, I studied course materials in preparation for the Chief Petty Officer/Quartermaster Examination that I would be eligible to take in November 1966.

***

Shirley and I settled into life in Ohio, finally reunited full time as a family. In May 1966, she gave birth to our third child, also named Kenneth. Life in the Puckett family had never been better.

At the same time, I began efforts to track down my birth father. In those days before Google, I sent out letter after letter to various government agencies, and I posted advertisements in newspapers throughout Kentucky, Ohio and Tennessee. Finally, I received an anonymous reply from one of my ads. The person wrote: "In reference to your ad, George Archey is now living in Rockwood, Tennessee."

It didn't take me long to make a solo drive south to the quaint little city of Rockwood, Tennessee, located about 75 miles west of Knoxville. It was somewhat economically depressed with only one motel. I booked a room there for the night before heading to the local barbershop.

Once in the chair for a haircut, I asked the barber if he knew George Archey.

"Yeah, I know George Archey," he said, as I recall. "He owns the building you're sitting in. His son is next door."

With that, he banged on the door to the adjoining office.

"Hey, Bobby, there's a guy over here who is looking for your dad," the barber said.

Bobby Archey came into the shop. I knew right away he was my half-brother because he was the spitting image of me. Our facial characteristics were very much alike.

"Hi, I'm Bobby Archey. I'm George's youngest son."

"I'm Ken Puckett."

The barber looked at me and looked at Bobby and said, "My God, this guy looks like he's related to you."

I didn't let on. I just said, "I'm looking for your dad. Do you know where he is?"

"He's out on the highway." His father was still an engineer building highways, now for the State of Tennessee. "He'll be home at 6 o'clock. Do you have his phone number?"

"Yeah."

"By the way," Bobby asked, "do I know you?"

"No," I said. "Thanks. I'll give your dad a call tonight."

Around 6, back in my hotel room, I dialed the phone. I heard it ring. A woman answered.

"Hello?"

"Hello. I'd like to talk to Mr. Archey," I said without identifying myself.

George Archey got on the phone.

"Yes."

"Mr. Archey, my name is Puckett. I've got some business I'd like to talk over with you. Could you come to the motel?" I gave him my room number.

"I'll be right there."

Fifteen minutes later, he pulled up in this Lincoln Continental. In the backseat was a woman accompanied by a dog. Everyone got out and came up to my room.

I immediately said, "Mr. Archey, I don't want to cause you any trouble. What I've got to say to you is between you and me. If you want to share this with anyone else later, you may."

He said, "I know who you are."

And the woman, his wife, Mayble, added, "If you got anything to say to him or do to him, you're going to do it to both of us."

I said, "I just need to know for my own purposes down the road who I am and who you are. I'm going to tell you a story about what happened about 25 years ago in northern Kentucky."

And she said, "I know what happened. George is your father."

"Well," I said, "then where the hell has he been for all these years?"

He said, "I've been around."

Mayble Archey looked at me and said, "You come home with me. You're one of my sons now."

I got into their car and went to their house and spent the evening with this family, including Bobby and a second half-brother. Mayble Archey and the two sons couldn't have been nicer.

We talked about a lot of things. The evening was cordial and pleasant until George Archey looked at me with a somewhat accusatory expression.

"What I'd like to know," he said, "is why aren't you using my name?"

For the first time that day, I lost my temper.

"You old SOB," I said. "Where have you been for 25 years? Where were you when I was living in poverty after my first stepfather was killed and my second one abandoned us? Why would I ever want your name?"

I learned later from one of my half-brothers that they thought I was going to punch him right there.

At that moment I realized that I could never reconcile with George Archey, that he was never going to be a father to me, even if he was flesh and blood. My great-aunt had warned me that the Archeys would never be my family. She was right. Too many years had passed.

I didn't really know these people. I didn't really want to know George Archey.

I left Rockwood that evening and never went back until 30 years later to visit my half-brothers. I'm now in contact with one of them and several nephews. They are all nice people, and they have helped me to understand the history of the Archey family.

Much later, the military helped me to officially change my name to Kenneth Paul Puckett. I felt I needed to do this to put distance between my birth father and me. But, more importantly, this made sure there would be no issues with my military records.

By the time of my trip to Rockwood, the clouds of war were beginning to cast a shadow over my seemingly bright future. The conflict in Vietnam was escalating, and those of us with quartermaster/navigator ratings were informed that the Navy could revoke our shore duty at any time and send us back to sea. I continued to work diligently on my education toward my goal of being selected for OCS.

I didn't know it at the time, but a very different career path was about to unfold.

5. The Army

As a Navy recruiter in Lima, Ohio, I worked out of a big training center where I shared office space with counterparts from the Army, Air Force and Marines trying to sign up young men for military service. I saw a lot of crazy things there. It was more than patriotism or paycheck that brought people to our door. More than once I had a woman come in and say, "Can't you take my son into the Navy? He's eating me out of house and home."

In those days we were given a minimum number of recruits we had to sign up each month. If we didn't meet our quota, the military could send us back to sea or to the infantry or whatever. I think my quota was two sailors a month.

The recruiters in the office looked out for each other. After I met my quota, I might say to a young man, "You don't want to go in the Navy. Why don't you go in the Army?"

On my desk I kept a photograph of a Navy tugboat. It was a visual reminder of my goal to get promoted to chief petty officer, become a commissioned officer and captain a tugboat – perhaps one of the heavy-duty seagoing rescue tugboats big enough for a crew of about 100.

One day in 1966, the Army sergeant sitting across from me looked up from some paperwork and said, "You know, Ken, I got a request here. The Army Transportation Division that runs Army watercraft –"

I interrupted.

"The Army has got ships?" I asked.

"Yeah, in World War II they had more ships than the Navy," he said, noting that the Army ran ships to transport personnel, vehicles, food and other cargo.

He continued explaining that the Army's watercraft division was gearing up for the Vietnam War by reactivating ships to help supply combat forces. But he said there was one problem: The Army didn't have enough senior people qualified to command the ships, so it was looking to poach qualified guys from the Navy and Coast Guard.

"How would they do that?" I asked.

The Army recruiter told me his branch would do it by initiating an "inter-service transfer."

It worked like this: The Department of Defense would transfer sailors and members of the Coast Guard who were qualified senior petty officers to the Army and then immediately promote them to warrant officer, a technical position between enlisted soldiers and commissioned officers. The newly appointed warrant officer would then go through an extensive Army watercraft operations training program after which he would be assigned as an operations officer or engineer onboard an Army watercraft. He would eventually move up the ladder to command Army watercraft and small ships.

Oh, the Army recruiter added quietly, an immediate assignment to Vietnam was inevitable.

I found that interesting, but I was happy in the Navy, especially because I was on a path to becoming a chief petty officer and eventually a commissioned officer.

But since the recruiters all looked out for each other, I agreed to sign a one-page form indicating my interest in transferring to the Army. This helped the Army recruiter fill his quota and, by doing so, he helped me get the equivalent of four signed Navy recruits.

Later in the month, I went before a board of Army officers who interviewed me. I signed off on another form, and that was that. I all but forgot about it.

In mid-1966, the Navy informed me I was eligible for promotion to chief petty officer. I had completed the practical factors and attended the advanced schools. I then only needed to pass the Chief Petty Officer Promotion Examinations. I guessed it wouldn't be long after that before I would be a chief quartermaster and then hopefully go to Officer Candidate School. I was so positive about my career advancements that I immediately headed to a military supply center in Columbus, Ohio, to put in an order for the appropriate uniforms for the higher rank I was certain would be coming soon.

While in the building, I spotted an Army procurement office and suddenly remembered that form I signed requesting a transfer. I decided to stop in and tell the Army to forget it before things progressed further.

I gave my name to a clerk behind a desk.

"Wait a minute," she said, pulling a card out of a file. "Where have you been? We have been looking for you."

She informed me that my request for an inter-service transfer had been approved and I would be joining the United States Army in 11 days as a warrant officer. Warrant officer? That sounded pretty good. Not only would I immediately move up in rank, but I also would eventually get to command a ship.

I went downstairs to the captain in charge of Navy recruiters and reserve training activities in Ohio and told him what I had done.

Of course, he flipped out.

"You can't do that," he said. "You got to go through the Navy to do that."

"No one told me I had to go through the Navy," I said.

"Let me call Washington," he said.

This was Thursday. The following Monday, I was given an airline ticket and ordered to fly to Washington to appear before a Navy board, which I thought would try to stop me from leaving. I was soon sitting in a hallway in the Pentagon with six other Navy guys who apparently had requested inter-service transfers to the Army.

I walked into a large room with a big, green-felt table. An admiral was seated at one end with several Navy officers on both sides. I stood at the other end, reported for duty, and then endured several minutes of feverish questioning, lengthy lectures and outright threats as the naval officers did everything they could to persuade me to cancel the transfer. They reminded me the Navy had approved my eligibility for promotion to chief petty officer with the possibility for Officer Candidate School. When I told them I still wanted the transfer, the admiral said he would make me refund my re-enlistment bonus – a threat he had to take back after a Navy Judge Advocate General officer at the table told him that wasn't legal.

At the end of the day, the Navy couldn't do anything about the departure of all seven of us. In fact, over the next two years, the Navy would lose another 150 senior petty officers/sailors who became warrant officers/soldiers in the Army Transportation Corps.

At 8 o'clock in the morning on October 19, 1966, I was released from the Navy after 8½ years of service. At noon the same day, I was sworn in as an Army warrant officer.

I wear my dress green uniform in a photo taken at the U.S. Army transportation school in Fort Eustis, Virginia.

I put on my new uniform and reported to the Army Transportation

Training Center at Fort Eustis, Virginia, for a six-month course on Army harborcraft operations.

***

My family once again joined me in a move to a new home in an unfamiliar place. Shirley did her best to cope with another relocation. I was around the family more. But my priorities had changed very little: They were now Army first, family second as I focused on adjusting to a new service branch while taking courses the Army transportation school.

***

In the Navy, sailors revere ships. A ship is such an intrinsic part of who and what you are in the Navy. The Navy carefully maintains its ships, knowing they can deteriorate very quickly even if they're not at sea. In the Army, I quickly discovered, a ship is another piece of equipment like a jeep or a tank. If a tank doesn't start, the Army goes out and starts another one.

While waiting for my training to finish, I got my first assignment as chief mate on a big Army harbor tug in Virginia. When I arrived at the tug for the first time about 2 o'clock in the afternoon, the only soldier I saw was on the gangway, smoking a cigarette.

"Where's the crew?" I asked him.

"Well, let's see," he said. "Four of them are at the PX, and four are in their bunks because they had a watch last night."

When I took a tour of the tug, I was shocked it was so filthy. I called everyone in and announced they would all be required to report at 7 the next morning, night watch or not.

"And fellows," I said, "we're going to clean this boat from stem to stern."

I thought I was going to have a mutiny on my hands. These soldiers weren't used to being pushed that hard. In a rear area, when the Army's not in combat, it really lets things relax until they go into training. I really had to change the discipline, and so did the other warrant officers who were transfers from the Navy.

But we were always running up against the Army's attitude that it could put a soldier anywhere. Even if he was an airplane crewman, the Army might give him a rifle and send him to the front.

I was sitting at my desk one day when an Army captain walked aboard.

"I need four of your guys for guard duty," he said.

"Wait a minute, it's my crew," I said. "I haven't got them fully trained."

"They work for you, but you work for me. Therefore, I'm taking them off your boat. You'll see them in three weeks."

This kind of thing went on for quite a while. I couldn't believe how the Army's approach to operating watercraft and ships was so inferior to standards of the Navy. Finally, I got fed up and requested a transfer back to the Navy.

The next thing I knew I was called into a meeting with Chief Warrant Officer Carter C. James, who headed the Army watercraft training programs. As we chatted in his office, I immediately liked the man. Mr. James – all warrant officers in the Army are addressed as "Mister" or "Chief" – welcomed me warmly and listened patiently as I spilled my frustrations.

Then, Mr. James proceeded to explain the Army system in a way I could understand. It turned out we had a lot in common. He served with the Navy during World War II; then, like me, he transferred to the Army's Watercraft Division where he became a harbor and docking pilot during the Korean War. After the war ended, he moved to the Army transportation school.

He had learned to live with the differences between the Navy and Army, and he assured me I could do so, too. He had reviewed my records and thought that I had a bright future with the Army if I chose to stay.

Mr. James then shared some important information with me: Once the Korean War was over, the Army cut its Transportation Watercraft Services by 75 percent. The result was, in 1966, even as the Vietnam War escalated, there were only 45 warrant officers remaining in the transportation corps qualified to operate watercraft. That's why the Army went to the Navy for personnel like me.

Then he said something that floored me.

"I will personally help manage your career," Mr. James said. "I will mentor you and see to it you have the opportunities you deserve."

I didn't need to hear any more. Never had anyone in the military, especially someone of such high standing, taken this kind of personal interest in me. I decided to stay with the Army, and I returned to my coursework with a positive attitude and purpose.

In April 1967, I graduated from the Army's Harbor Craft Deck Officers Course with honors.

Then, before I had much chance to savor the accomplishment, I received new orders. I was going to Vietnam.

6. Vietnam

IN May 1967, a jet door swung open, and I stepped out into an alien world of palm trees, paddy fields, roaring helicopters, rock music and extreme weather. This was Vietnam. Every place in that country was a war zone. I had never seen or felt anything like it in my life. The biggest shock was the heat. It was like walking into an oven – a scorching dry heat that almost made it hard to breathe.

A few days before, I had dropped Shirley and the kids off in her hometown of Nelson, British Columbia, where she had the support she needed from her Canadian family. In California, the Army put a bunch of us from the watercraft school together as a unit, and we boarded a Trans International commercial cargo jet contracted to fly to Vietnam, our M-16s and .45s stowed below us in the cargo bay.

After a stop in Hawaii for refueling, we landed in Vietnam and reported for duty. Immediately, all of us new warrant officers were dispersed to various areas. They just sent us wherever we were needed.

Incredibly, in my unit, we had a couple of young privates who said jokingly, "I want to be an infantryman." The Army said, "Grab a gun. We'll see you."

I soon arrived at the 97th Heavy Boat Company, 125th Transportation Command, in Cam Ranh Bay, where the Army had a major cargo and port operations base. I was assigned to be a "mate" – in this case, the second officer – on Army harbor tugboat LT-1940. Our assignment was to assist ships in and out of the port and to move various cargo barges throughout the bay port. (On ships, the Army calls its captains "masters" and its junior officers "mates." Army watercraft and ship officers are ranked as warrant officers; the pay grades at that time went from WO1 through CWO4. I know, it's all very confusing.)

As for the heat in Vietnam, I adjusted quickly. After two or three weeks, I found myself enjoying it. I just had to remember to drink a lot of water. When the monsoon season came in full force in July, it was still hot, but now everyone got wet for more than three months. It was rain, rain and more rain for days on end. I learned in Vietnam that you were either hot and dry or hot and wet.

During this tour of duty, the U.S. had more than 480,000 troops deployed in Vietnam. By the end of 1967, the war's death toll for Americans would climb to 11,100 as the U.S. escalated its support of the South Vietnamese and their fight against communist-controlled North Vietnam and its Viet Cong guerrilla forces.

Army transportation watercraft crewmen didn't stay in one place too long during the war. The minute someone got a little experience and seniority, the Army moved him.

In July 1967, a colonel re-assigned me to be captain of LCU-1559, a Landing Craft Utility that ran cargo up and down the Vietnamese coast to ports too small for larger ships.

The LCU had living facilities for two officers – myself and a chief engineer – and 13 crew members. We typically carried about 170 tons of cargo. It could be trucks, it could be food, it could be ammo. And we would run supplies into little ports all up and down the coast. But it was a very slow vessel; we only did 8 knots (about 9 miles per hour) as we traveled along the ocean. It would take forever to get anywhere. The ship, which was used during World War II and the Korean War, was designed to take cargo from a ship to port in an hour, then go back and get more cargo. It was not designed to do what we were doing.

All in all, it was a good assignment. I liked captaining the boat as it was independent duty. However, the first time we pulled into one

In 1967, I stand on the beach in Cam Ranh Bay, Vietnam, in front of the LCU-1559. The vessel was an Army landing craft utility with a crew of 12. This was my first "command" of a vessel with the U.S. Army 24th Transportation Battalion.

of these little ports to dump off cargo, bullets began bouncing off our hull. The enemy was attacking. We fired our machine guns a little, things quieted, and we unloaded the cargo without anyone getting hurt.

We learned to move quickly and to keep our heads down. That kind of attack would happen a lot when we went into a port. It seemed the North Vietnamese always knew when we were coming. However, I ordered my crew not to engage the enemy unless it attacked us first.

"We're not combatants. That's the job of the Army Infantry and the Marine Corps," I told them. "Our job is to supply them with the equipment they need. You keep the portals closed and don't try to be a hero. You could kill (North Vietnamese leader) Ho Chi Minh himself and I'm not going to give you a medal. Don't do something dumb. I want you guys to go home alive."

In any case, we all knew that hauling cargo was nowhere as dangerous as the situations faced by the guys who were out in the field in direct combat.

***

In November 1967, I was promoted to chief warrant officer WO2 and reassigned as second officer on the U.S. Army vessel John U.D. Page, named after a colonel who died in the Korean War. The Page was a Beach Discharging Lighter (BDL), which was the only really large ship the Army had at the time: It could carry up to 60 half-ton trucks on its main deck or 25 to 30 tractor-trailers. It was designed to go out to special Navy ships, off-load vehicles and then move ashore into shallow water and discharge the vehicles on the beach. It also traveled up and down the Vietnamese coast delivering military cargo.

But whoever designed the BDL must have been a Navy guy who had it in for the Army. It was designed with a cycloidal propulsion unit. It was like having eggbeaters on the stern. The design made the ship very maneuverable, but it was slow. The BDL also had this bow ram that was supposed to push us off the beach, but all it did was dig a hole.

The captain of the John U.D. Page at that time was kind of a character. He was made captain because he was a very senior Army warrant officer who had been in the field for a long, long time. However, his last assignment aboard a vessel was in Korea.

A problem we faced with these types of landing craft cargo ships were the Vietnam tides, which would rise and fall about 10 to 16 feet every six hours. In June 1968, we came to a coastal beach at high tide to discharge cargo. I reminded the captain that we needed to move quickly before low tide or we could be grounded on dry land, which at night made us extremely vulnerable to enemy attack.

On the deck of the U.S. Army Vessel John U.D. Page on January 20, 1968, that's me on the far left I was being promoted to Chief Warrant Officer W2. Also pictured are CWO Carter C. James, second from left, and Lt. Col. Franklin John Glunn II, battalion commander, right.

"Don't worry about it," the captain told me. "We'll be in and out in two hours."

As I feared, we were still on the beach when the tide went out, and we got completely grounded. It was so bad we could have gotten off the ship and walked all the way around it.

Amazingly, the captain and chief officer decided our beaching was a good time for the crew to paint the ship's hull. I told them, as it was growing dark, we should focus on getting the rest of the cargo unloaded. They ignored my opinion.

There were further delays, and we were stuck on the beach until 3 a.m. waiting for the next high tide. While the rest of us watched for the enemy, the captain and chief officer headed to the officers' club on the beach to have a few drinks.

As the tide became to come in, we noticed a bunch of lights in the

I stand in front of the LCU-1559 at Phan Thiet, Vietnam, after the tide went out and we were beached for about four hours.

water behind the ship. We checked them out and determined they were just Vietnamese fishermen with tiny lights floating in baskets.

Just before 3 o'clock, the captain and chief officer returned, and the captain noticed those lights on the water. Before we could stop him, he grabbed a machine gun and started firing at the them. It took several seconds before we were able to get him to stop. I'm not sure whether he hit anyone, but those lights in the baskets sure went out in a hurry.

I was furious. "Look, I may be a junior guy here," I told the captain, "but you shouldn't have done that."

He said, "You're fired. I'm kicking you off the boat."

"Fine," I said. "I'm gone anyway."

With that, I took the opportunity to inform him that my tour of duty was scheduled to end, and I was rotating back to the United States.

***

My mentor, Mr. James, had been pleased with my work in Vietnam, and he had arranged for me to be assigned to an Army transportation unit in San Francisco. I was made the captain of the Army vessel U.S. Army Vessel Resolute. My mission: put the Resolute, a 460-foot-long cargo ship, into operation for training Army Reserve personnel in cargo operations and longshoreman duties.

The Navy had pulled the Resolute out of its dead fleet and turned it over to the Army Transportation Corps. The ship was towed to Treasure Island Naval Base in San Francisco and tied up. Previously, the ship had been known as the USS Pembina. Some guy at Army headquarters in Washington decided to rename it Resolute.

After picking up my family in Canada and moving to the Presidio of San Francisco, a military post, I reported for duty.

The Army promised to assign a crew of soldiers to the Resolute, but weeks and months passed without a crew. I did get six vehicles from the Army, but no one to drive them. I had one civilian assigned to me as my maintenance guy.

Day after day, I'd go down to the ship, turn on the telephone, make a pot of coffee and just sit there with this dog that I adopted after I found him wandering the pier. I basically had nothing to do except walk around the base and kibitz with people. Then I'd go home at night.

This went on for about six months with no security, no lookouts, no lights and no crew for the Resolute, even though the Army was paying the Navy rent for this pier space.

Eventually, the Navy brass got fed up. The base commander called me one day and said, "For security purposes, you can't have a ship tied up at my pier without anybody there at all times."

"I don't have a crew," I told him. "I'm not going to sit onboard that ship 24 hours a day. At night I turn off the shore power, lock the gate on the gangway and go home. I have approval from my commanding officer to do so."

The Navy base commander refused to accept my response and requested a meeting with my superiors and me at the 6th Army Headquarters. I was pleased with this development, as I hoped the meeting would result in the Army giving me a crew.

I'll never forget the experience of seeing a fuming Navy admiral confront an unresponsive Army general.

"Look," the admiral said, "you can't park a ship like it's a tank, and then walk away from it. It's got to have a crew."

The general shrugged. "Well, it's not going anywhere."

The admiral stood up and put his hand on the table and started pounding it.

"Damn it," he shouted. "A ship is a living thing. It moves. It's got *a soul*."

The general finally turned to me.

"Chief, what do you need?"

"Right now, I need security."

The Army still didn't give me a crew right away. But it hired a Pinkerton guard to do a watch on the ship.

Not long afterward, a San Francisco newspaper editor, who was in the Army Reserve and happened to be at the meeting, wrote an article about the dispute, accompanied by a poem, which I committed to memory:

The Resolute, the Resolute,

A mighty ship is she,

With a crew of one,

And engines dead,

She can't put out to sea.

The Army doesn't want it,

The Navy's in a stew,

'cause she hasn't got a berth,

And she hasn't got a crew.

The tide comes in,

The tide goes out,

She bangs against the pier,

While faces of the Navy men,

Show signs of total fear.

But Puckett will scrape it up,

And paint it good and

Make it look so neat,

The Army will be proud it had

That ship in its stupid little fleet.

I was an instant celebrity in San Francisco after that newspaper story ran. But I still had no crew.

Bored, I did things just to rattle cages. I began wearing my Army military fatigues to the Navy officers' club, which had a rule that officers had to wear a semi-dress uniform. When I was told to leave because I was "out of uniform," I explained that wasn't possible.

"I'm the commanding officer of my ship, and I've prescribed this as my uniform."

The Navy fumed but couldn't do anything about it.

Finally, things began to pick up. All sorts of shipments began arriving, including coils of new mooring lines. It looked to be a clear sign the Army was finally ready to give me a crew.

Then the Resolute began getting shipments of food. I had no place to store it. I had no refrigeration. I called the Navy supply office and was told, "Don't keep the perishables more than three days." So, I began giving it all away. People from the Navy base would come over to get meat, doughnuts, cakes and fresh loaves of bread.

During this time, I was sitting on the deck of the Resolute having coffee when around the end of the pier came this big, white, beautiful ship. It tied up on the other side of the pier across from me. Then I saw the name on the bow: U.S. Coast Guard Cutter Resolute. That's when I realized that the Army had named my ship without bothering to see if there was another one in the U.S. fleets with the same name.

Before long I received an invitation from the other Resolute's commanding officer. He had noticed the coils of new white line and supplies next to my ship and demanded to know if any of that "stuff" belonged to his Resolute.

"I think we got a problem," I said.

We eventually learned how the mix-up in shipments had occurred: The Coast Guard's Resolute had been due to arrive four weeks earlier. After it was delayed, someone failed to notify the Coast Guard's supply department. When all these supplies began arriving for "the Resolute," everyone at the Navy base assumed it was for my ship.

We ended up reaching some financial settlement with the Coast Guard. The Army really didn't care about the cost. The Vietnam War was still going strong, and no one seemed to worry much in those days about money.

Finally, I got a small unit of Army reservists assigned as my crew – but only on weekends. But they worked hard, and we got the Army's Resolute clean and operational.

***

As I grab one of the mooring lines to the Army Vessel Resolute, Lt. Commander Johnson, armed with large pair of scissors, "cuts" it as the ship is kicked out jokingly at the U.S. Naval Base on Treasure Island in San Francisco in 1970. The ship was soon moved to Hunters Point in San Francisco. (U.S. Army photo.)

Just as I got settled into a good routine with the Resolute, in June 1970 the Army ordered me back to Vietnam. I was assigned again to the 124th Transportation Port Command in Cam Ranh Bay. Once again, I was placed aboard the John U.D. Page. By then, though, there was a different captain and mostly a different crew.

I wasn't in that job for two months when I got a call from Mr. James, now the Army harbor master responsible for port operations in Cam Ranh Bay.

"Ken, I think it's time we moved you up," he said.

Mr. James explained that he wanted me to work directly for him as a channel, harbor and docking pilot. I was eager for the assignment but told him I was a little surprised because I was still junior to many of the warrant officers stationed there. Becoming a ship pilot was a premier assignment and a position I knew most of the other warrant officers in the watercraft field wanted.

"You seem to have the ability to move ships. I trust you will get the job done," Mr. James told me. He also mentioned that, unlike some others, I didn't drink, and I always had a positive attitude. "You're not a prima donna," he said.

By 1970, most of the South Vietnamese working as pilots had been assassinated by the enemy, who sneaked south and killed them in hopes it would hinder U.S. cargo deliveries. By the time I became a pilot, there were no South Vietnamese pilots, except in the Saigon River. The few Vietnamese pilots still working were put under protective guard.

I received three weeks of pilot training, which was all I needed to do the job because I had been in the system and was qualified as a tugboat captain and ship captain. The training didn't involve any classroom instruction. We just went aboard the ships with the other pilots until they felt we were qualified to work as a pilot. With that, I was certified by the Army as a harbor and docking pilot, and I started bringing ships in and out of Cam Ranh Bay.

For the next nine months, I piloted more than 600 ships of all sizes, including cargo vessels and petroleum tankers in Cam Ranh Bay. I also visited several other locations along the Vietnamese coast to set up port operations and institute pilot training for others. It was grueling duty involving long hours under constant alert and combat conditions. The three of us Army harbor pilots worked around the clock. But I loved it, even during times I went days with hardly any sleep. I'd get off one ship and immediately move to take another.

Cam Ranh Bay in the early 1970s was a beehive of activity with a large South Korean infantry division on one side of the bay and a large Army compound on a hill on the other. The harbormaster and harbor pilots had their own house along the water so we could get on ships right away when needed.

Even though we were in a war zone, life in the bay was mostly peaceful. However, we did have several incidents in which the Viet Cong sent swimmers into the harbor at night to plant satchel charges to try to blow up ships. The Navy eventually brought in dolphins trained to detect the enemy swimming underwater. It was a super-secret operation at the time.

I was on duty at Cam Ranh Bay for about a month when I piloted a ship loaded with ammunition. While doing that, we were told two Viet Cong swimmers were spotted hanging off the bottom of the pier, apparently stranded when the tide went out. They had just grabbed onto the pilings and hung on while trying to hide.

Instead of shooting them, an order came through to send Navy divers on a patrol boat to flush them out. This operation went on long enough that the tide came in and the two let loose from the pier and started to escape underwater. Our fear was they still might try to use explosives against one of our ships

I ordered our ship to go into reverse toward the pier to block the enemy's escape. Before I realized what was happening, the ship propellers literally sucked these two Viet Cong out from under the pier and right into the blades. All that was left were pieces of the two men. It was the worst thing I'd ever seen in my life. I never did learn if they still had explosives on them.

***

Vietnam had hazards we didn't completely understand at the time. I was working in a port when two C-130 airplanes came over the bay and sprayed something on the jungle nearby.

"What the heck is that?" I asked someone.

"They're blowing Agent Orange," another soldier answered, referring to the chemical defoliant that the U.S. military was using to kill vegetation and other cover used by the enemy. "They're trying to quickly clear an area of foliage, so they can create a helicopter landing pad."

I kept my eye on this for a while. Suddenly, the wind blew the wrong way. A bunch of us got hit with a wave of this spray. I knew getting soaked by an herbicide wasn't good for us. But at the time, like most Americans there, I knew almost nothing about Agent Orange other than I had to off-load 55-gallon drums of it from ships. We knew it was Agent Orange by its orange markings on the barrels. I often had to tow barges loaded with Agent Orange for delivery to the Air Force.

Years later, veterans would learn that exposure to Agent Orange caused a wide range of illnesses. Uncounted numbers of us would suffer from leukemia, Hodgkin's disease, Parkinson's disease, diabetes, prostate cancer and other illnesses. Some even saw their toenails fall off.

Everybody who served in Vietnam – even those on Navy ships off the coast – was exposed. More than two million Vietnamese, mostly civilians, also have suffered from the chemical. What we did in Vietnam with Agent Orange, in my view, was the biggest crime in the world. The stuff was that nasty. And there was no recovery from it once you were exposed.

During my second tour of Vietnam, I became very disillusioned in many ways. I saw clearly how badly things were going in the war. I noticed how corrupt the military had become in ways largely hidden to the American people at the time. There were so much waste and a lack of focus on the part of our armed forces. One example: The military set up a retail automobile dealership there so guys could pick the car they wanted when they came back to the States. That's the kind of bizarre stuff that went on. I was relieved when my second tour ended in July 1971.

After this, I was assigned to the Army Transportation Watercraft section of the Washington State National Guard in Fort Lewis, Washington. I was responsible for training National Guard units and for overseeing maintenance of Army watercraft on the West Coast.

I did that for less than six months when I heard again from the Pentagon about taking another assignment.

7. Japan, Korea and the Philippines

I received a phone call in January 1972 from the Army Transportation Command. A colonel got on the line. He got right to the point: He wanted me to volunteer to go to Okinawa on a six-month assignment to supplement the harbor piloting operation there.

The Americans had occupied the island of Okinawa in Japan since the end of World War II. But in the fall of 1971, after years of pressure from the Japanese, the U.S. signed a treaty agreeing to return Okinawa to Japan the following July.

Since the 1940s, the U.S. Army had employed Americans in Okinawa as ship pilots, harbor pilots and docking pilots, but they were all civil service. When the Okinawa treaty was announced, some of the American harbor pilots quit or retired. After a dispute over wages, some still on the job began a work slowdown. This put the Army in desperate need for pilots – and that's why the colonel was asking me to go to Okinawa.

I knew the Army already had several senior warrant officers in Okinawa with piloting experience. I asked the colonel why some of them weren't being tapped for this assignment.

He said he would get back to me, then hung up.

Within 10 minutes, the phone rang again, but this time the caller was Chief Warrant Officer Carter C. James. My mentor was back from Vietnam and living in Virginia.

He explained to me how port operations in Okinawa had come almost to a standstill. At one point, more than 75 ships sat at anchor because there were too few pilots. Mr. James said senior warrant officers in Okinawa refused to volunteer for pilot duties because they didn't want to be at odds with civilian pilots or to jeopardize their futures in the civilian shipping industry.

Because of my seniority and qualifications, James told me, he handpicked me for this assignment.

When I got to Okinawa in early 1972, the situation was even worse than I had feared. As the only military person assigned to piloting, I was essentially blackballed by the civilian pilots; they refused to train me or to offer any guidance. They didn't want me there, and they had friends who backed them up. One night I was at a restaurant when two guys attempted to beat me up. I could only speculate who sent them. Fortunately, two Marines stepped in to protect me.

For a long while, I sat in the Port of Naha with nothing to do. Then out of the blue, I got an assignment to pilot a ship owned by a New Jersey shipping container company. I happened to know its civilian captain from my tours in Vietnam. When I climbed aboard, he sympathetically told me I had to leave.

"I'm sorry, Ken, but I can't take you," he said.

"What are you talking about?"

He said the company had sent him a message not to take a military pilot. "They named you in particular," he said.

As I went back down the gangway and onto the pier, a jeep pulled up. An Army colonel stepped out.

"Where are you going, Chief?" he asked.

"Well, I can't take the ship out because the captain won't let me. He won't let me take it off the dock."

The colonel said, "I'm ordering you back aboard that ship."

"That's an unlawful order, Colonel. The captain won't let me handle the ship. Get one of your civilians to do it."

"You either go back aboard that ship or I'm going to charge you with direct disobedience of lawful orders," he said.

I knew at that point that I had been set up.

"Go back aboard," the colonel said.

"Sir, I can't."

"Then you're under arrest. Get in the jeep."

I had no choice. I jumped in the jeep, which whisked me to my living quarters. The colonel then ordered me confined there until further notice. He even threatened to put an armed guard outside my door. I couldn't believe that I had volunteered for this mess.

Fortunately, I had an ace on my side. The first thing I did was telephone Mr. James in Virginia. "Let me make a few phone calls," he said.

The next morning, I got a knock on the door. It was an Army major who was chief of staff to the three-star general in charge of Okinawa.

"The general wants to see you," he said.

I got in a sedan and headed for the meeting. As I stood before the general, he told me he knew nothing about my situation, other than I had been arrested.

"Sir," I began, "just put me on a plane and send me back to the States. I'm disqualifying myself as a pilot. Get yourself another guy, General, because I'm not putting up with this."

"Settle down," the general said quietly. "Have a seat and explain to me what is going on."

I went through the whole story of how I had volunteered to help the Army get ships moving again, but civilian pilots and Army supporters were trying to intimidate me into leaving.

"What can we do to straighten this out?" the general asked.

"You fire everyone down there you can, you put me in charge as harbor master, and I'll move the ships," I told him. "I'll take every ship from 8 in the morning until 10 at night. I'll put those civilian pilots back to work. If they refuse, we suspend them."

The general not only agreed with my plan, he immediately cut orders to that effect. He also assigned me an armed driver. He wrote a letter to the New Jersey shipping company that said, in effect, the way it treated me was not acceptable.

With the authority of the general behind me, port operations in Okinawa turned around almost overnight. Faced with suspension and losing pay, the civilian pilots went back to work. I opened the harbor to traffic after sunset, but I refused to give the pilots the overtime. I personally took everything after 4 o'clock in the afternoon until 1 o'clock in the morning. Toward the end of the assignment, the Army sent another warrant officer-pilot to assist.

***

During my downtime, the Army asked me to take a temporary assignment to captain a 140-foot seagoing tug from the Philippines to Okinawa while it towed a large barge stuffed with military equipment. In those days we didn't have sophisticated satellite weather systems like they use today. Instead, the second mate had the responsibility of picking up weather charts before we sailed. I didn't know until it was it too late that the charts he picked up were three days old.

We left port and got in a channel between northern Luzon and the mainland of China when a typhoon hit. It got rough with seas 45 to 60 feet high. We just tried to keep the bow into the weather and hoped the storm would soon pass.

The barge was a mile behind us when the cable suddenly parted. We rode out this typhoon for two and a half days before it finally blew over. Not long afterward, about six miles off our starboard side, we spotted the barge. It had ridden out the storm along with us. We reconnected the barge and took it to Okinawa as planned.

It was one of the worst storms I'd faced since I was on the Valley Forge. I was still young in 1972 when the typhoon struck, and I didn't think much about how much danger I was in. It was only when I got older that I thought more about what a risky place the ocean can be. Even now, with additional safety systems, there are ships lost every year carrying lumber from the coasts of Oregon and Washington. You don't hear much about it, but they get out there – sometimes overloaded on top with lumber – and sink, losing not only the cargo but the crew as well.

In Okinawa, Japan took over everything as scheduled on July 1, 1972. I was the last U.S. military ship pilot to work there. Before I left for the States to be reunited with my family, a Japanese admiral came in, shook my hand and gave me a set of cufflinks.

***

The next two years were one of relative stability for the Puckett family. When I came back to the States, I was transferred to Virginia for an advanced warrant officers course, and I graduated with honors.

Mr. James soon informed me that the Army had opened its college-degree completion program to warrant officers and that he had chosen me to take part. In January 1973, I moved with my family to New York and began studies at the State University of New York Maritime College in the Bronx. While an undergraduate, I was appointed to be assistant dean of students as well as assistant varsity basketball coach. By the end of 1974, I had my bachelor's degree in marine transportation management.

***

In January 1975, the Army sent my family and me packing again, this time to South Korea. I was assigned as chief of port services, with responsibilities that included being harbormaster at the U.S Army Port in Pusan. We settled in and put the kids in school.

Over the next two years, Shirley put in more than 1,000 hours of volunteer work as chairwoman of the 25 volunteers who operated an American Red Cross office in Pusan. She told the *Stars and Stripes* newspaper that she had been looking for work to "give me something constructive to do." She led volunteers who provided reading assistance to school children, delivered baked goods and books to remote sites, helped blood drives, and provided orientation for new arrivals.

In 1976, the Red Cross awarded her its Clara Barton Award for her volunteer work. I was extremely proud of her.

In Pusan, I supervised more than 500 South Korean maritime personnel employed by the U.S. Army. I also had 14 active-duty Army personnel working with me.

For years and years, the U.S. port operations had a great working relationship with the South Koreans, especially the civilian ship pilots. When the U.S. military needed a pilot, it called Korean port authorities, who would assign a pilot to handle a ship. The Army would ask how many tugs and what marine equipment the pilot needed to handle a ship movement, and the U.S. provided the support and coordinated the operation.

However, in February 1976, the Korean Pilots Association announced it purchased five large commercial tugboats. It then notified me that its pilots would no longer be using our Army tugboats. Instead, they would use their own tugs and charge us for the service at a rate of an additional $1,000 an hour. The pilots claimed our Army tugs were old, underpowered and unsafe. But we knew better. It was true our tugs were a little old, but they were in excellent condition. This was just a money grab by the South Korean pilots.

We suddenly had a crisis. The U.S. government hadn't budgeted for this additional tug expense. Switching over to these South Korean pilot tugs also meant laying off our tug captains and crews. We tried to negotiate this issue with the South Korean pilots, but they refused to budge and instead shut down their piloting service to the U.S. Army ports.

The Army then agreed to my suggestion to allow me to personally pilot the four to six ships a week at our ports in Pusan and Masan, South Korea. I would pilot more than 120 ships between July 1975 and March 1977. The South Korean pilots were not happy with me, but they couldn't do anything about it.

As planned, the U.S. soon turned over control of its port operations to South Korea, which then had to deal with their pilots.

***

I was assigned in summer of 1977 to the U.S. Army Advisory Group in Fort Lewis, Washington, where I was the marine maintenance officer for all Army watercraft on the West Coast.

In 1978, I spotted in the newspaper that the newly created Panama Canal Commission was looking to hire pilots and other personnel. The canal was searching for qualified applicants after the U.S. signed the 1977 treaties to begin the transition of canal operations to Panama, with full control handed at the end of 1999.

Almost immediately after the treaties were signed, there was this cadre of American workers, pilots included, who quit or retired. Many others refused to take part in training Panamanians, whom they knew were in line to be their replacements.

Faced with a shortage of pilots, the canal put out the announcement it was looking for Americans who had Merchant Marine licenses or captain's licenses, and who were also qualified ship-handlers. The commission had about 55 to 60 slots open for pilots.

Having already contemplated retirement from the Army, I sent in an application to the Panama Canal Commission. Before long, it sent Port Captain John Meeker and two other senior pilots to Seattle to meet piloting candidates. They interviewed me at a hotel and gave me a questionnaire to be completed and returned the next day.

When I came back, one of them said, "Okay, you're on the final selection list. We'll let you know." Because they also told me they had 1,600 applicants for those 55 to 60 pilot jobs, I left and didn't really think much more about it.

Then on July 31, 1978, I finally did it: I retired from the military. It seemed like the right time to do so. I was age 37 with a good pension and what I knew were great qualifications to succeed in the civilian shipping business. Every license I received in the Army Transportation Corps was comparable with merchant industry licenses and requirements. Plus, I had my college degree. Better yet, I had a standing offer to go to work with a company in the Philippines to manage its shipping and seafood operations.

When I retired from the Army, as a routine matter, I was sent to the Veterans Administration for a physical evaluation and entry into the VA's medical data systems. VA doctors determined I had high blood pressure as well as some depression caused by my experiences in Vietnam. I didn't request a disability rating because I still wanted to work and thought it would hurt my access to jobs in the maritime industry. Regardless, the VA awarded me a disability rating of 10 percent and authorized a small disability check.

After that, I immediately accepted a job and signed a contract with the shipping company in the Philippines, once again bringing Shirley and the kids with me.

Right away, I discovered how naïve I was about working for a private company operating in a foreign country. I did a terrible job looking out for my family when I signed that contract. I was looking at the money instead of the impact the job and place would have on the family. I was away at all hours, focusing on company business.

Within six months in Manila, I wanted out. About that time the Philippine government decided to nationalize our company's seafood plant operations. I realized it was only a matter of months before the whole business would collapse.

I went to work one morning, and I got a call from one of the Filipino bankers saying that the government was going to take our company. Rather than just walk away, my Filipino manager and I closed out all accounts and paid 125 employees six months' advance pay. We dismantled the plant on a Friday, and by Sunday my family and I were on an airplane to the United States.

***

In 1979, Mr. James called to say he received a message for me to call the Panama Canal Commission. I soon learned that the commission had officially approved my application to be an apprentice pilot. I immediately accepted the offer and began shipping our furniture to Panama.

Shirley had different ideas. She had been talking to a Seattle friend who had lived in Panama with her husband. The woman painted a horrifying picture of conditions there, including the long rainy season, snakes and scorpions. She further suggested that security was deteriorating as Panama took over the former U.S. Canal Zone. Shirley's friend thought Panama was the worst place in the world. After that, there was no convincing my wife to move to Panama.

Shirley said it was my choice to take the job, but that doing so would be the end of our marriage. We had moved 12 times in the previous 16 years, and she was tired of it. She also determined that our children needed some stability. For the first time, Shirley stood up for herself and the family when it came to one of my job moves. And for the first time, I made a career decision based on what she wanted.

"Well, then," I said, "we won't go."

I informed the folks in Panama I couldn't accept the job offer, and I began looking for work in the Seattle area. By now our assets were being depleted rather quickly. We were living in a hotel – and I still had to get our furniture back from Panama.

"Maybe you should go back in the Army," Shirley said.

"I'm not going back in the Army," I said.

Then, I sort of did.

One morning in February 1979, Karen picked up the *Seattle Times* and read that the Army Corps of Engineers in Portland was operating ships that dredged the rivers and harbors on the West Coast. Karen looked up from the paper and said, "Maybe you could get a job with the Corps of Engineers, Dad."

God bless my daughter. The next day I drove to Portland, where I applied for any maritime position the Corps had open. It didn't matter whether it was as a seaman, deckhand or watch officer. I needed work.

Within a week, I was offered a mate's position aboard the Army Corps of Engineers dredge Biddle. I was back in business.

We moved to the Portland area. Again, my family life took on some stability. But after so many exciting jobs in the military, I found life on a dredge to be a drudge.

Just before Christmas 1980, I had lunch with an old Army friend who told me he just accepted a job as a Panama Canal pilot. He mentioned that the canal commission was having trouble bringing in qualified American pilots because the wages were well below industry standards. But the commission had come up with several incentives to lure pilots. Among them was the option of a "six/four" schedule where a pilot would be on-duty full time for six weeks, then have four weeks off to fly back home to the United States.

Just for the heck of it, I called the Panama Canal personnel office and asked about the program and wondered what the process was for re-applying for a pilot job.

A personnel officer put me on hold for a moment and then reconnected.

"Captain Puckett," he said, "the application you submitted in 1978 was approved. You were selected as an apprentice Panama Canal pilot then; therefore, I see no reason for you to have to apply again."

Then he added, "When do you want to come to Panama?"

I told him I needed to discuss this with my wife, and I would let him know our decision.

"Give me a call when you work out the details and I will send you the necessary papers," he said. "Have a nice Christmas, and I hope to see you the first of the year."

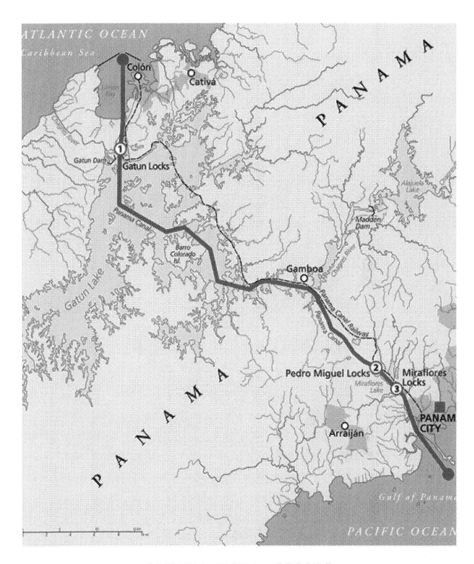

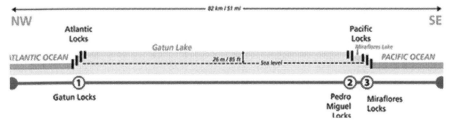

This map of Panama shows the route of the canal built by the United States and the multilevel design of its locks. (Map courtesy of Shutterstock.)

8. A Man. A Plan. A Canal: Panama

AFTER a lot of discussions, Shirley agreed I should take the job on the Panama Canal and then commute to the State of Washington every six weeks. She would stay in Vancouver with the children. We would try to make this work.

In a sense, I owe a debt of gratitude to a bullying tactic of President Theodore Roosevelt for helping me to get the job. To understand that, I'll share another brief history lesson.

There had been talk for centuries about building a canal in Central America, but it wasn't until construction in the 1860s of the Suez Canal – which allowed ships to travel from the Red Sea into the Mediterranean Sea – that people really began thinking they had the technical capability for a canal across Panama. Such a shortcut meant ships no longer would need to take the long, perilous route around Cape Horn on the southern tip of South America to go from New York to San Francisco.

At the time, though, Panama was a state in the nation of Colombia. After a bidding competition, Colombia in 1875 granted a concession to France to build a canal across the narrow strip of land known as the Isthmus of Panama. To head the project, France hired Ferdinand de Lesseps, the same engineer who built the Suez Canal.

De Lesseps was full of optimism January 8, 1882, when work began on the Panama Canal. What he didn't realize initially is that a canal across Panama was not the same as building the Suez Canal. All he needed in the Middle East was some bucket dredges to dig a 300-to-400-foot-wide ditch through sand. He didn't need locks to raise and lower ships because the Mediterranean and the Indian Ocean are both at sea level. And, more importantly, there was no mountain range to cut through.

De Lesseps had decided he could duplicate the Suez Canal design in Panama. All he needed, he thought, was enough money and manpower.

His initial design for the Panama Canal was to be 150 feet wide and 26 feet deep, cut through vast jungles and through the mountain range that is part of the Continental Divide.

However, De Lesseps quickly ran into major obstacles.

The first was the weather. It rains somewhere in Panama almost all the time, especially during the summer months. Steady precipitation would prove to be a positive thing later when the United States built a canal with a lake-fed lock system that needed rain to replenish the watershed. But during French construction, rain was always getting in the way, washing everything out and causing frequent landslides.

His second problem was geology. Panama is a geologist's nightmare. It has 17 different types of rock. For de Lesseps, the Continental Divide proved to be an overwhelming obstacle. He couldn't dig through its major rock formations with bucket dredges.

The third thing de Lesseps underestimated was the toll tropical diseases would take on construction workers. France did clean out all the jungle areas where diseases thrived. But cholera, malaria, yellow fever and dysentery continued to be so virulent that some people would be working on the canal one day, and the next they would be dead. According to one report, some watched as their own coffins were brought into hospitals so that their bodies could be quickly removed to make room for other patients.

French digging of the canal finally halted for good on May 5, 1889, with 70 percent of the excavation completed, after financing for the project collapsed. By then the project had lost $287 million, which in today's dollars would equal about $14 billion. At least 27,000 people lost their lives working on the project due to disease, construction accidents and other causes.

***

Around this time, America's ambitions as a world economic and military power were growing. By the turn of the century, business and political leaders wanted to expand America's land and sea forces to defend itself and its interests. But the U.S. Navy faced a major dilemma: If it needed to move a battleship from one coast to the other, it had to contend with a 14,000-mile journey around South America. A canal through Central America would shorten the trip to around 5,000 miles.

Because of the French failure in Panama, many in the United States favored building a canal in Nicaragua. The conditions in Panama – the disease, the geology, the rain, the difficulties in recruiting construction workers – didn't disappear after the French disaster. President William McKinley and his vice president, Theodore Roosevelt, were among those initially favoring Nicaragua. But after McKinley was assassinated in 1901 and Americans began to take note of volcanic activity in Nicaragua, Roosevelt put his considerable energy behind a canal in Panama. For many, Roosevelt's personal stake in the Panama Canal fits perfectly with the world's most famous palindrome: "A Man, A Plan, A Canal: Panama" – a phrase that reads the same in either direction.

Roosevelt offered Colombia $10 million for the rights to build the canal in Panama. When Colombia rejected that amount as too little, Roosevelt backed a revolution by Panamanians for an independent country. He then pressed the newly formed nation of Panama into signing a treaty giving the U.S. a huge swath of land in Panama and the rights to build a canal that America would own in perpetuity. For that, the U.S. paid Panama $10 million upfront, plus rent of $250,000 a year.

Simply put, Roosevelt bullied Panama to get what he wanted, and nobody likes a bully. There would be bad feelings for decades between the two countries over this deal that gave the United States the canal under such favorable terms.

President Theodore Roosevelt sits on a steam shovel in Culebra Cut during a visit to Panama on November 15, 1906. (Library of Congress photo.)

In 1905, the U.S. created the Panama Canal Company to construct the "Big Ditch" and to operate it. One of the first things it did was establish an American controlled Canal Zone that was 10 miles wide and stretched 54 miles long across the Isthmus of Panama.

Roosevelt appointed John Wallace, a railroad engineer, to oversee the construction, which still had the problem of disease and death. When Wallace moved with his wife to Panama, they arrived with two metal caskets, one for him and one for her. I imagine it didn't do much for the morale of workers

Wallace tried for months to get construction going. But every time he had to buy something, he had to get approval from the Panama

Canal Company located 1,200 miles away in Washington, D.C. Finally, after about year and a half, Wallace quit in frustration.

Roosevelt next turned to John Stevens, a railroad construction engineer who had the nickname "Big Smoke" because it always seemed he was smoking a big cigar. Stevens declined the job until he was given assurances he would have enough money, manpower and, most important, the authority to make decisions without running every time to Washington. Roosevelt agreed to give him the autonomy, and Stevens took the job.

Stevens sent recruiters all over the world to find workers. Meanwhile, he built roads, housing, sanitary facilities and commissaries. He said, in effect, "I'm not going to start the canal until I got decent areas for people to live and work."

Taming Panama's deadly diseases was his initial priority. For that, Stevens turned to Major William Gorgas, an Army medical officer. Gorgas suspected that the two main diseases – yellow fever and malaria – were being borne by mosquitoes. He convinced Stevens to allocate 2,000 men to drain pools of standing water in ditches and to spread oil over water to kill larvae where mosquitoes were breeding. He had screening systems installed to keep mosquitoes out of homes and hospitals. Within a year, the rate of deaths in Panama due to malaria and yellow fever went down to next to nothing.

Stevens figured out that a sea-level canal would be too difficult to construct. He chose instead a plan to dam the Chagres River, creating an artificial lake at 85 feet above sea level that ships would cross between a set of locks. Using water from the lake to fill their chambers, the locks would then raise ships to the level of the lake and then lower them back to sea level at the other side.

He had the locks designed with double lanes side by side so that two ships could simultaneously go in either direction. Each chamber was made 1,000 feet long, 110 feet wide and 42.5 feet deep – dimensions built to U.S. Navy specifications so that its biggest ships at the time would have sufficient clearance.

Stevens got everything going and then, in 1907, in the midst of construction, he resigned. Roosevelt was furious. He had given Stevens everything he requested, and he still quit before the canal could be completed.

This time, Roosevelt appointed Colonel George W. Goethals of the U.S. Army Corps of Engineers to finish supervising construction of the Panama Canal. Roosevelt had given up on civilians for the job. He knew that, if Goethals decided to quit, Roosevelt had the authority to order him to stay on the job.

Goethals seamlessly took over where Stevens left off. He didn't change the basic plan. And he not only saw the canal to completion, he stayed as governor of the Canal Zone after the SS Ancon made the first official transit of the canal on August 14, 1914.

In more ways than one, the U.S. construction of the Panama Canal proved costly. America spent upward of $370 million on the project, including a payment of $40 million for French interests. More important, an estimated 5,600 workers lost their lives during construction.

As the years passed, the canal became increasingly costly to operate. Civil service salaries grew. The government also provided employees with low-cost housing, highly trained security, excellent schools and well-stocked places to shop. The food and other goods in the canal commissaries were vastly superior to what could be purchased anywhere else in the country. Few Americans realized that the Panama Canal Zone had become this utopia, with U.S. taxpayers footing the bill.

Naturally, native Panamanians resented how their own people lived in poverty while Americans in the nearby Zone enjoyed a luxurious lifestyle.

In 1946, Panama asked the United States to hand over the canal. The U.S. refused, in effect saying, "We signed a treaty with you giving us the canal in perpetuity. That means forever."

In 1956, when the U.S. backed Egypt's demands to take control of the Suez Canal from France and England, Panama insisted the Americans similarly turn over the Panama Canal. The U.S. again pointed to the treaty that stated the U.S. owned the canal in perpetuity.

The issue again surfaced in 1964 when riots broke out in Panama. Twenty-six Panamanians died, and approximately 16 U.S. military personnel were seriously injured. Communist agitators had begun making inroads in Panama by stirring anti-American sentiment over ownership of the canal. Still, the United States insisted it would hold onto the canal in perpetuity.

By the 1970s, the value of the canal to American military forces vastly declined as more of its vessels became too large to fit through the locks. U.S. leaders finally began talks about handing over the canal to Panama. In 1977, the U.S. and Panama signed treaties to turn over the canal to Panama in a transition over the next twenty-three years. The two countries formed a Panama Canal Commission to carry this out.

U.S. President Jimmy Carter and Panamanian General Omar Torrijos sign the Panama Canal treaties in Washington, D.C., on September 7, 1977. (Photo from the U.S. National Archives.)

The treaties, while wildly popular in Panama, drew immediate fire from Republicans and their right-wing supporters back in the United States. Scores of Americans working for the canal and their families also were livid. For many, the Canal Zone was the only home they had ever known.

As many workers began quitting and others threatened sickouts and other disruptions, the commission needed an insurance policy to ensure it had enough qualified workers.

That's where I came in. The commission decided to include six military veterans, including me, among 35 newly hired pilots in 1980 and 1981. It knew that, under the terms of our previous military service, the U.S. had the option to order the six of us back on duty until we reached age 62.

"We can treat you like Roosevelt treated Goethals," I was told by a canal manager sometime after I was hired. "If you quit, or just look at us cross-eyed, we can throw your butt back in uniform."

He said this to me in a joking way, and I don't think the U.S military would have done it, but that's the threat he put out there.

***

Want to read more about Theodore Roosevelt, the history of the Panama Canal and some related topics? I recommend these four books:

- *The Fourth Part of the World: An Astonishing Epic of Global Discovery, Imperial Ambition, and the Birth of America*, by Toby Lester. It's a heck of a history book about cartography.

- *Mornings on Horseback: The Story of an Extraordinary Family, a Vanished Way of Life and the Unique Child Who Became Theodore Roosevelt*, by David McCullough. I don't think *Mornings on Horseback* is a great title for a book, but it's a fascinating read about Roosevelt's family, from the time he was a small boy into adulthood.

- *The Path Between the Seas: The Creation of the Panama Canal, 1870-1914*, also by McCullough, is nearly 700 pages long and can be a challenging read. But it's the most definitive book about the construction of the canal and American ambitions at the time.

· *The Greatest Generation,* by Tom Brokaw, is a very interesting take on those who served in World War II and how this generation that came of age in the 1930s and 1940s shaped modern America. A lot of what I describe in this book is best understood in context with the stories Brokaw tells.

9. The apprentice

IN January 1981, I flew into Tocumen International Airport in Panama. Captain Donald Garrido, a longtime pilot, picked me up in a sedan and delivered me to temporary quarters in a hotel in Panama City. For the next two weeks, I settled in, had a physical with necessary inoculations, and spent time becoming familiar with the Panama Canal Zone. Then I began my apprenticeship.

The Pilots in Training program was unbelievable. Spanning about 19 months, the training was – and still is – the most intensive and expansive in the world for ship pilots. The Panama Canal Commission didn't just assign pilots to move ships through the canal. It also trained them to bring ships up the channel to the harbor and the canal, and to work as harbor docking pilots in Balboa, Cristobal and the U.S. Naval Base Rodman.

The core of my training involved making at least 195 "transits" – one-way crossings of the Panama Canal, both day and night – initially under the supervision of a senior pilot. Nothing better prepared someone for piloting a ship than the actual experience of maneuvering ships up the channels, into the locks and across the lake.

After 19 months, if successful, I would become a Step One pilot able to work solo on ships 525 feet long and about 75 feet wide. Then every year after that, management would evaluate my performance and decide whether to approve me as a Step Two pilot, then Step Three and so forth. The final step would be Step Eight, which was the level of a "senior pilot" qualified to work on any ship.

The training included hundreds of hours of classroom instruction along with numerous hours shadowing employees in various jobs on the canal. The commission wanted to make sure that once we became pilots and started requesting certain support systems or operations, we would know what the people assisting us were doing. In 1981, the canal employed about 8,000 people, mostly Panamanians.

I trained on canal tugboats for a couple of weeks. The tugboats, as they still do, assist ships into the locks and escort them through the canal.

I also spent time learning about the diesel-electric locomotives that hold ships off the walls when the pilot brings a ship into the locks. The locomotives, also known as "mules," run on an electric Hot Wheels-like track along the length of the original lock walls. The locomotives use cables attached to ships to keep vessels in the middle of the chambers and off the concrete.

I also spent time with the dredging division, which kept the canal clear of debris from mudslides, especially along the Gaillard Cut, the 700-foot wide man-made valley through the mountains. (Panama in 2000 returned this landmark to its original name, the Culebra Cut.)

Every time we turned around, the mountains were caving in. In 1986, we had an earthquake that caused a major slide that took almost a year to dig out.

At the Marine Traffic Control Center, I learned how it scheduled ship transits. Every ship was supposed to take about an hour and a half to get through a set of locks. If a pilot took three hours to do that, one fewer vessel went through that day. This, of course, resulted in a loss of tolls to the canal. (Tolls were charged vessels based on their size, cargo and other factors. When I started in 1981, the highest toll ever paid was $89,154.62 for the cruise ship Queen Elizabeth II. The lowest was 36 cents paid by Richard Halliburton in 1928 when he swam the canal.)

I also spent weeks monitoring the lock control houses that lower and raise the water in the locks, and that operate the huge gates. The

A Panamax-size bulk carrier, assisted by Panama Canal tugs, passes three dredges working to remove debris from a major landslide that occurred October 13, 1986. (Photo from the Panama Canal Commission 1986 annual report.)

biggest vessels allowed through the canal then were called "Panamax," which meant they were at the maximum size to pass through with sufficient clearance on all sides. Over the years, as ships grew larger, fewer operating on the world's oceans met that standard.

Each lock was built with a series of steel gates weighing 390 to 730 tons each. But because they are hollow – sealed off at the bottom and airtight – they float on the water just like a ship. In fact, they're so perfectly balanced that each can be opened and closed with a 25-horsepower motor. When we trained, we were shown how to open and close a gate with a crank. It took forever, but one could crank it by hand in case of a power loss. We could do it with just human muscle because these dog-gone things are so perfectly balanced.

The locks also use what's called "mitered gates": The edges are angled so that the pressure of the water on one side makes them seal tightly. If the edges came together 90 degrees straight across, the seal wouldn't hold. You know who first designed mitered gates? Leonardo

The Guia, a Panama Canal tug, aligns the Panamax-size container ship Ever Gleamy as it prepares to enter the locks. (Photo from the Panama Canal Commission's 1989 annual report.)

Da Vinci back in the 15th century. He designed them for locks in Europe.

As part of my training, I had to literally commit to memory the entire 50 miles of the canal waterway, including channel widths, water depths, pier and berthing lengths, vertical clearances, locations of lighthouses and buoys, and bridge heights. I had to understand tide changes and wind directions and how to maneuver various types and classes of ships in the canal.

I discovered very quickly that the Panama Canal has its own unique navigational quirks. For one thing, the tides get much higher on the Pacific side than on the Atlantic/Caribbean side. There is basically no tide as ships enter from the Caribbean – maybe 6 inches to a foot. On the Pacific side, there's a 14-to-18-foot tide that changes every six hours. These tides are created by the Peruvian current, the rotation of the earth, and the pull of the moon and the sun on the waters of the Earth.

Understanding the tides is key to Panama Canal piloting. The tides greatly affect the movement of water on the southern entrance. These vertical movements of the water going up and down cause horizontal movements that can make it difficult to steer a ship.

Another unique aspect of the Panama Canal is the mixing of saltwater and freshwater as ships enter and exit the locks on the Pacific side. Water from Gatun Lake flows through the Cut, enters Pedro Miguel Locks, then moves across Miraflores Lake into Miraflores Locks before flowing out to sea. Freshwater floats over saltwater and causes surface movement.

Adding to that are tides that oppose the freshwater currents from the locks. Thus, a ship may be in both saltwater and in lake water. This mixing causes an undulation of current that affects the ship laterally. In ship-handling, left to right movement is what you try to avoid. When you start to go sideways, you have very little control. It requires someone with a tremendous amount of ship-handling experience to handle a ship in waters that are moving in different directions at the same time.

When we wanted to pass a vessel going the other way on the lake, we could do so with a clearance of 75 to 150 feet, depending on the size of the ship. In the case of the largest ships, only one at a time was allowed in the narrow channels. Two large ships passing each other too closely creates a suction effect, resulting in the potential loss of control.

One thing most people don't realize is that the Panama Canal does not run east and west. Don't believe me? Look at a map and you'll see the canal runs mostly north and south because the alignment of the Isthmus of Panama is on an east and west axis.

A typical transit for me as an apprentice began in the morning around 6. I would meet up with one or more of the primary or "control" pilots and board a launch that whisked us to a ship.

The most dangerous part of a transit was climbing the pilot's ladder up to the ship's deck. Often, it would be 40-foot rope ladder with wooden rungs draped over the side of the ship. These ladders were almost always covered with oil and grease due to their storage conditions. Throughout the world, every year, at least two pilots suffer serious injuries boarding ships on these ladders.

As a pilot got older, difficulty in climbing that ladder would often be a factor in deciding to retire or to find another assignment on the canal. In those days, if a pilot became ill, could no longer transit or didn't want to do so anymore, he was permitted to move into a management position, such as port captain or training officer.

As we boarded the ship, the control pilots and I would immediately head for the bridge, where one of them would assume navigational control of the ship. The Panama Canal is the one waterway in the world where the captain of the ship was required to relinquish complete control of his ship to the pilot. From a small yacht to the largest vessel – even Navy submarines – a Panama Canal pilot is in full navigational control of the vessel while transiting the canal.

***

During my apprenticeship, I was assigned one day to a German cruise ship with a German-speaking captain. Our senior pilot that day was a native of Germany who had obtained his U.S. citizenship. That was not so unusual. We had 26 different nationalities among the pilots. Most had obtained U.S. citizenship because, until the 1977 treaties, one had to be an American to be one of the 240 pilots on the Panama Canal.

This German-born pilot soon got into an argument with the German captain. I'm not exactly sure what they were fighting about since they both were speaking German, which they weren't supposed to do. The conversations with Panama Canal pilots were always supposed to be in English. I couldn't do much about it anyway as I was just an apprentice.

This argument continued as we were going through the Gaillard Cut. As we neared the Pedro Miguel Locks, the captain shut down the engines. We began to drift.

I looked behind us. I could see that we were in trouble. The ship was sliding sideways. In such a situation, it's easy for the crew in the wheelhouse not to notice, especially on a big vessel such as a cruise ship. The bow may seem to be in the correct position while the stern could be crabbing on a 45-degree angle. That's exactly what was happening with this German ship. The bow was going to clear the entrance to the locks, but the stern was heading for the bank.

"Hey, skipper," I said to the pilot, "you got to look behind you, because –"

The pilot interrupted me.

"I don't need you to tell me what to do," he said.

And then the German captain piped up, finally speaking in English: "Mind your own business. We're busy right now."

I said, "Really?" About that moment, the stern slammed the bank of the canal. The impact severely damaged the ship, including the rudder.

I don't know if the German ship captain was disciplined over this accident. However, I do know that two days afterward, the German-American pilot was back at work. It was as if nothing happened.

Even if he had lost his job, the pilot had zero legal and financial responsibility for the accident. When a pilot put his hands on a ship, he became a contractor, a semi-employee of the ship working under the auspices of the captain. And if he made a mistake, he was not personally liable.

When I was on the canal, there were an average of 32 accidents a year. Not bad considering the pilots put thousands of ships through during that period. But any pilot who said he never had an accident is lying. All pilots on the Panama Canal had incidents in which they dented a ship or landed heavily on the wall. Things happen.

Think about it. It's difficult to park your car in the garage when the kids' bicycles are on both sides. Imagine what it's like to get a ship through the narrow portions of the Panama Canal while battling lateral movement of the vessels, high winds, swirling currents of water and other unpredictable conditions. In theory, scraping the wall wasn't supposed to happen because we had tugboats and locomotives along the locks to keep a ship in the middle of the canal. But accidents occurred because everybody involved was trying to do his own thing.

If an incident occurred on the Panama Canal that required repairs, the captain anchored his ship and filed a report. He called his company, and it hired a marine surveyor from a certification society to inspect the ship. It was the surveyor's job to say if the ship was seaworthy.

Within two hours of the incident, lawyers representing the company were required to notify the Panama Canal if they were going to file a claim for damage. The canal's Board of Local Inspectors would then hold a hearing within six to eight hours of the incident. A very senior pilot was chairman of this board; he would take possession of the ship's logs and would gather testimony from those involved. The purpose was to have people testify right away so they wouldn't have time to make up a story.

After a hearing, the board knew 85 to 90 percent of the time what had really happened. The case was typically settled within 48 hours because time is money with cargo ships. Everybody got a copy of the hearing testimony, and a decision was made on compensation and whether to discipline the pilot or anyone else. During the time I was there, we had pilots resign after they had a bad incident.

It is a fine line between a mistake in judgment and negligence. As a pilot, you never wanted to cross that line.

***

After I completed 35 transits as an apprentice under close supervision, the canal allowed me to handle some piloting duties on bigger ships. At the same time, I was given solo assignments piloting yachts and small fishing vessels.

In this photo scanned from the Panama Canal newsletter The Spillway in 1984, I peer out from the observation deck at the Miraflores Locks as the cruise ship Island Princess approaches.

When I started piloting, a pilot was required to complete that transit whether it took 10 hours or 14 hours. Later, the canal changed that rule due to fatigue factors. The pilot's union said, "Look, after eight hours, we got to relieve these guys." Shorter work days meant more pilots were needed to handle the workload. When I was there, we'd burn through 40 to 50 pilots a day.

In summer 1982, I had completed 190 training transits, shadowed other employees, and finished classroom requirements and other components of the official training program. Now it was time for the written exam that involved drawing from memory all seven navigational charts of the Panama Canal. It took a week to take the exam, and I passed it on the first try.

I also was given a "check ride" in which I successfully took a ship through the Panama Canal as the control pilot. In November 1982, I was issued my Step One license. I was now a full-fledged pilot.

Not everyone in the apprentice program succeeded. Of the 35 new apprentices when I came aboard, eight of them for various reasons did not complete the program.

10. Night transits

My first transit after receiving my license as a Step One pilot was an assignment aboard a small Japanese refrigerated cargo ship. I was told to arrive at the ship at 6 p.m. for an overnight transit that would be completed about 8 the next morning.

The night before, I went out celebrating with four others who also just became Step One pilots. I didn't drink, as usual, but I stayed out with the group all night. When I returned home, I remained awake all day as I got organized for the assignment.

I arrived promptly at the ship. After a brief delay, I navigated it through Gatun Locks, clearing it about 11 at night. By the time we started south on the 19-mile trip across Gatun Lake, the ship's captain had gone below, leaving a third officer up there alone with me.

When a pilot is aboard a ship, he normally does very little work in the sense of putting his hands on the controls. It's the ship's officers who steer according to the pilot's instructions. Unless the pilot sees something out of the ordinary or the ship must make an abrupt turn, he just allows the crew members to do their jobs. He might make some minor adjustments such as "Come over left a little bit" or "Come right a little bit" or "Stay on course."

As the Japanese cargo ship headed across the lake at half-speed, I relaxed and enjoyed the ride. I settled into the captain's chair to take in the view. I thought: What a beautiful night. And then, to my everlasting embarrassment, I closed my eyes and fell asleep.

The Japanese third officer continued at the controls as if nothing happened. Despite the darkness, he expertly steered the ship across

Gatun Lake. He knew enough to keep his eyes on the channel buoys and other navigational aids. In short, he did one heck of a job.

When the ship neared Gamboa, the city where the Chagres River meets Gatun Lake at the entrance to the Gaillard Cut, he gently shook me.

"Excuse me, Pilot. Do you want me to take the ship into the Cut or do you want to take it?" he asked.

"Oh, my God," I said, jumping up from the chair.

I immediately realized my negligence. If there had been an incident, that would have been it. That would have been the ballgame. I would have been fired. If there had been damage to the ship, the Panama Canal Commission would have had to foot the entire repair because it would have been 100 percent my fault.

Now, wide awake, I picked up the captain's chair, walked out to the bridge wing and threw it over the side.

I went back and took over piloting for the rest of the journey.

As I was getting off after the transit, the captain came up to the bridge. We shook hands, and he said, "Thank you very much, Pilot. Here's a bottle of sake." I guess he didn't know or didn't care about my nap – or his missing chair, for that matter.

I said, "Thank you very much, Captain," Then I handed the present back to him, a gesture that seemed to puzzle him. The truth was, I was extremely embarrassed and just wanted to get off the ship.

But I took time to turn to the third officer and hand him my pilot's cap. It was my way of acknowledging him. "Mr. Mate, you earned it," I said. "Thank you very much."

For the next 15 years and through more than 1,000 transits of the Panama Canal, I never again sat in the captain's chair. Never.

***

Usually, I enjoyed transiting the canal at night. It was quieter. The temperatures were cooler.

But navigationally the night offered its own special challenges on the Panama Canal. When the temperature cools to 65 to 70 degrees Fahrenheit, heavy fog comes in. I could be halfway across the lake when suddenly it appeared. The only electronic aid I had to navigate at the time was radar. Fog at night could get very scary.

Lighting at night was an issue, too. During the first 50 years of the canal, it operated only during daylight because of the lack of lighting. In 1964, the canal installed a bank lighting system throughout the locks using posts with a cluster of six 1,000-watt lamps. Still, pilots complained it was too dark at night to take big ships through safely.

Depth perception was an issue, too. If we had been in a rowboat, it wouldn't have been a big problem. But when elevated as we were on the ship's bridge, we could see objects farther away, but our depth perception and ability to guess visual distance was skewed.

The higher we were, the closer objects appeared to us than they really were. It was an illusion caused by the fact that our eyes take in images upside down; our brains make them look right side up. But it doesn't always get the depth perception right. To compensate, in the old days of sailing ships, the lookouts in the masts of the vessels would hang upside down to trick their brains to make it appear they were on the surface of the deck of the ship, and that way they could see how close things really were.

When I taught ship-handling, some students wouldn't believe this effect until I showed them. From the deck of a ship, I'd ask them to guess their distance from a buoy. They'd say it was a few feet away. Then I'd tell them to bend over and look between their legs. They thought I was crazy until they did it and saw clearly that the buoy was 100 yards away.

Today, pilots have Doppler radar and other equipment on board. They don't rely as much on visual cues to know their location. Even so, depth perception is still a problem.

Consequently, cruise ships in Miami seldom come in at night. They'll arrive in early morning, not because they want to meet the

8 o'clock schedule, but because it's a difficult job to move a ship at night.

Sometimes when I took a ship through at night, the captain and crew would go nuts because they thought we were too close to the bank, when actually we were 100 yards off. I never faulted them for that mistake. They weren't used to the canal, and they weren't trained to adjust their minds and their visual cues.

Add speed to the equation, and nighttime transits became even trickier. The speed of the ship at night appears a lot slower than the same speed during the day. Someone on board who wasn't monitoring the equipment might think the ship was going 2 knots when it was really at 4 or 5.

Transits became easier at night when, in the mid-1980s, the Panama Canal Commission installed modern high-mast lighting. It improved visibility for smaller vessels and allowed more night transits by larger vessels. These tall towers have powerful lights that cover a wider area, fill in shadows and help with depth perception.

You might think the pilots were happy when the canal put in high-mast lighting. However, the Panama Canal pilots' union argued that pilots deserved additional compensation because the new lighting meant they would be sent on more of the riskier nighttime transits.

I couldn't believe the union was complaining. I said to one of the union guys, "Wait a minute. It's safer." But that wasn't necessarily the union mentality. Its priority was always to figure out how to get more money any time the commission changed the pilots' way of working.

Sure enough, we soon got a bonus of four extra hours of pay every time we took a Panamax ship into the entrance locks before sunrise or remained in the exit locks after sunset. I used to joke the canal could have saved money by turning out all the lights and have no night transits at all.

11. Water buffalo

O NCE I got to Step One, my relationship with the senior pilots improved quite a bit. The anti-apprenticeship attitude toward me faded as I worked my way up through the system. During this period, I made an effort to introduce myself to Panama Canal office staffs. I tried to meet everybody, including the administrator of the canal, retired General Dennis P. McAuliffe. Some ex-Zonians didn't like McAuliffe. A few even referred to him behind his back as "General McAwful" because they resented the growing loss of privileges for Americans and his work to integrate Panamanians into the workforce.

A few months after I became a Step One, I got a call from the port captain, John Meeker, with an assignment. John, one of those who interviewed me in Seattle when I applied for a piloting job, was among the best Panama Canal pilots and merchant mariners I have ever known. He was also a gentleman and just a nice person.

Anyway, that day I was a little surprised he called. It was not typical for the port captain to call a pilot directly with an assignment.

"Ken, how are you today?"

"Good, Captain Meeker. What can I do for you?"

He asked if it were true I was from Kentucky.

"Yes, I grew up there."

Then he asked me about my military background, about being in both the Navy and the Army and the inter-service transfer, and about my piloting assignments in Asia. This went on for a few minutes. The questioning seemed a little odd because he had been on my selection board and had to already know that information.

"Well," he said, finally, "with your credentials, we've got a ship for you. It's a ship only you can handle."

That sounded good to me. As a Step One pilot, I didn't expect to get any especially important assignments, certainly not one in which I had any specific qualifications.

John didn't offer much about the assignment. All he told me was that the jitney would pick me up at 5 a.m. the next day for a northbound transit.

The next morning, I put on a nice pair of slacks and a crisp white shirt, as well as my pilot's cap, making sure I looked my best before I stepped into the launch. I saw I was the only pilot aboard.

The high-speed launch Ballena is seen in this photo from the Panama Canal Commission's 1988 annual report. The launch was designed to rush personnel between work stations along the canal.

The launch headed out into Panama Bay on the Pacific side of the canal. We kept going and going until I wondered whether we somehow had missed the ship.

Finally, I could see a strange-looking object anchored in the distance about seven miles out of the bay. The launch operator pointed to the vessel. "That's it, way out there," he said.

By now the sun was coming up. In the growing light, I noticed that the configuration of the hull wasn't like anything I had seen before.

It looked like a cargo ship, but there were four open decks all the way up and down.

And then I noticed a stink. Not a mild odor, either. More like the stink from the outhouse I used growing up. Only worse.

I climbed the pilot's ladder with the stench only getting stronger. On the bridge, I met the captain and crew of the Philippine ship. I also noticed two Australian guys hanging out.

"What are you doing here?" I asked the two men.

One said, "You'll find out."

I turned to the captain. "What kind of ship is this?"

"It's a cattle carrier," he said. "We're carrying 1,600 head of live water buffalo from Borneo to Cuba."

The reason for the shipment was that Borneo was modernizing its farming, getting rid of water buffalo it used for generations to help with the sugar plant basins. These water buffalo were being sent to Cuba to work the sugar plantations there.

I learned the vessel had been traveling the Pacific under a hot sun for 26 days while its cargo of 1,600 cattle pooped all the way. It was a not-so-little ship of horrors.

By now the odor was almost making me sick. The whole ship stunk like you wouldn't believe.

Right about then I got a call on the radio from John Meeker, who had trouble containing his mirth.

"You know how I asked if you were from Kentucky?" he said. "That's why I thought you're the only one qualified for the job."

I laughed. I guess John thought all Kentuckians raised water buffalo or something. (Over time I became good friends with him and his wife, Edith, who worked in the canal port operation offices on the Atlantic side. Edith made a point to take special care of what she called "my pilots," and, like John, she was highly respected by those who worked with her.)

The two Australians on the bridge eventually revealed they were veterinarians hired to keep the water buffalo alive over the 26 days at sea. They said their biggest challenge was making sure the cattle had enough fresh water.

But neither they nor I had the worst duty aboard that ship. You might imagine how much poop was produced by 1,600 water buffalo. The Filipinos were working 24 hours a day, seven days a week just shoveling it over the sides.

"You know," one of the veterinarians told me, "we wouldn't get lost if we had to turn around and go back to Borneo. We just would follow the trail of poop."

The veterinarians were in incredibly good spirits, probably because they left Borneo with 40 cases of beer. They told me they had consumed almost every one of the 960 cans. In Panama, they planned to stock up more.

"That means the two of you each drank an average of 18 cans of beer a day?" I asked.

"Pretty much," one said, "although we did share a few cans with some of the crew."

When we got to Balboa, the ship's agent came aboard to give everyone their mail, handle some paperwork, and load food and additional supplies, including 24 cases of beer.

We transited north through the Pacific locks without delays, but then waited three hours in the lake before we could start through the Gatun Locks. The whole time, pilots on ships downwind were complaining over their radios about the odor. And it only got worse as the poop built up on deck because the crew couldn't just shove it into the freshwater lake.

The ship finally arrived in the Caribbean Sea and headed north. I imagine it left a trail of poop all the way to Cuba.

12. Coal ship

IN December 1984, I was assigned to the M.V. Panamax Star, which was scheduled to pass through the Panama Canal with 55,000 tons of coal and a 20-member crew of Chinese and Burmese sailors.

When the 790-foot-long ship arrived, it was at "maximum draft" due to its heavy cargo. In other words, the bottom of the hull wasn't allowed to go any deeper than 39 feet 6 inches to safely transit the canal, and that's what it was at when it started to come into the locks.

I boarded the Star with three other pilots; it needed two control pilots and two bow pilots because the ship was so big. I noticed the place was a mess. There were plants growing food in the wheelhouse. The captain and crew looked scruffy, some with hair down to their waists.

Not long after I arrived, the two control pilots told the other assisting pilot and me, "Go down and get your breakfast." We headed to the mess hall and put in an order for breakfast with the Chinese cooks.

As we were sitting there, I noticed in the corner four American guys dressed in red jumpsuits.

"Hey, guys, what are you doing here?" I asked.

"We're firemen," one answered.

"What do you mean you're firemen? Why would they have firemen aboard a coal ship?"

The guy just smiled and said. "Well, you don't need to know."

By now, the ship was well on its way through the Gatun Locks. The two control pilots had put it through the first chamber and were entering the second chamber when I hurried to the bridge.

I told the control pilots, "There's something wrong. This thing has got four firefighters aboard."

One of the control pilots immediately headed for the mess hall, where he confronted the firemen and finally got answers.

Three years earlier, the Panamax Star struck a coal pier on the Mississippi River and caused $2.2 million in damages. In March 1984, the vessel was detained by the U.S. Marshals Service in Baltimore after a terminal operator in Louisiana filed a lawsuit in federal court to collect damages. By then, the Star had been loaded with high-sulfur West Virginia coal for shipment to Taiwan.

As a legal fight ensued, the ship was forced to anchor in the Chesapeake Bay off Annapolis for nine months. Its crew remained stranded on board while hoping the Taiwan Power Company, which owned the coal, would put up money to allow the ship to sail. None of the crew wanted to leave, fearing if they left the ship they wouldn't get paid. Crew members estimated each was owed about $25,000 in back pay, according to news accounts in the *Baltimore Sun*.

In October 1984, a Panamanian-based shipping line reportedly bought the Star at auction for $1.25 million, and the crew agreed to a settlement to receive most of their back pay and to continue aboard to the Far East.

Meanwhile, all that coal sitting in the cargo began to develop "hot spots," which were gaseous pockets where spontaneous combustion might occur. The U.S. Coast Guard found readings of 150 degrees in some parts of the cargo. If the coal got hot enough, the whole thing could go up in flames, or even explode, sinking the ship.

A marine firefighting firm from Texas was called in to repack the coal in hopes of eliminating air pockets. The ship's crew also welded the cargo hull shut and put taps on it to allow injection of special chemical fire deterrents in case this coal mass got out of control. The ship owner's insurance company placed firefighters aboard to monitor the cargo during its voyage.

By the time the ship reached Cristobal, the temperature of the cargo was being measured at 200 degrees, so hot you couldn't place your bare hand on the hold.

Once we learned of this, we knew that ship shouldn't pass into the Panama Canal. If the Star got onto the lake and caught fire there, firefighters would have to dump water in the cargo hold. The ship would likely sink, as it was already at maximum draft, and all that high-sulfur coal would pollute the water. Of course, it also would be a mess trying to pull the wreckage out.

One of the control pilots put in a call to the port captain. "Look," the pilot said, "we got a dangerous situation here that we weren't told about." He explained the discovery of the overheated cargo.

"Well, you'll have to pull the ship out, because you can't continue," the port captain said.

That wouldn't be an easy task. The power of ships in that era was limited, especially in reverse. A single screw vessel can lose up to 70 percent of its power efficiency when backing. The propeller was simply not designed to go in reverse.

We used the limited engine power and the canal's eight locomotives to slowly move the ship back out of the locks. Once we reached ocean level, we opened the gates, put a tugboat on the stern, and used its power and the power of the ship's engines to move the Star completely out of the locks. It was a very tenuous situation, as we had to be extremely careful not to damage the ship's hull.

Once out of the locks, we put two additional tugboats on the ship and towed it backward for six miles to Cristobal Harbor. We reached an area in Cristobal wide enough to turn the ship around. We cast off the tugboats, and soon the ship was headed off to sea.

We were told later that the crew took the ship on a two-month voyage south around the tip of South America to get to the Far East. They somehow managed to arrive without catching fire.

This incident was the kind of thing that happened from to time when ship owners tried to hide the truth so that they would be allowed through the canal.

13. A hole in the gate

I took a ship with a Polish crew into the Panama Canal locks in 1985. Nothing seemed out of the ordinary. We were going about 2 to 3 knots into the chamber when I said to the captain, "Stop engines." And he stopped the engines.

Then I said, "Put the engines half-astern." That meant for him to move the ship backward.

And he said, "Oh, Captain. Engines no-go astern."

"What are you talking about? Put the engines astern."

He said, "They won't go astern. They haven't gone astern for two months."

"Why didn't you tell me this until now?" I asked.

"I didn't want you to know, so you would not refuse to take us through the canal."

I said, "You're an idiot."

About the time I said "idiot," we ran right into a gate. We couldn't stop. While we were cabled to the locomotives, they weren't designed to stop a 60,000-ton ship. They are meant to help slow it down and to try to keep it in the middle. We relied on a ship's engines to move the vessel inside the canal.

When we hit the gate, we poked a hole, causing a spray of water. Fortunately, there are two sets of gates. The second gate kept the entire lake from draining into the ocean.

Somehow, we got the ship under control. Doing the best I could with the malfunctioning engines, we finished the transit without further incident and got the ship out of the canal.

For weeks afterward, every time I'd arrive at that same lock in the morning, the lockmaster would call me. "Is that you Captain Puckett?" I'd say, "Yeah, why?" "Oh, we just want to let you know we didn't patch your hole yet."

Of course, it wasn't my hole. But for three months, I had to live with being the pilot who "poked a hole in the gate."

***

I piloted a 400-foot ocean trawler with a Soviet crew coming back from Antarctica. It was at night, when we often let smaller ships through. I was assigned to the ship just a few hours before I went aboard.

The captain was a nervous ninny about going through the canal. He seemed scared to death that there was going to be an accident and that perhaps he was going to get in trouble for it back home.

We were about three hours into the transit and ready to go through the chambers when he started saying, "We're heading into the locks. We're heading into the locks," like we're going to crash, even though we were fine.

Suddenly, he turned the ship, making a hard right a full 90 degrees. Sure enough, we ran into the bank. We were stuck in the mud just because he panicked.

"What the heck did you do that for?" I asked.

"I don't think it will fit through the canal."

I said, "Look, your ship is 75 feet wide and it's a 110-foot-wide lock. We can get through there."

I had to get tugs to pull us off the mud bank before we could resume the transit. Fortunately, there was no damage to the bow.

***

By the mid-1980s, many of the pilots were in a confrontational mood with management and were regularly complaining about safety issues on the Panama Canal. Their complaints focused on inadequate lighting, confusing buoy signals and scarcity of firefighting equipment. Some observers, including Panamanians, thought that U.S. maintenance of the canal had deteriorated since the treaties were signed.

In 1985, a tanker crashed going through the locks and spilled water ballast from its cargo hold over one of the diesel-electric locomotives that guided ships. Pilots shuddered at what might have happened had the ship's normal cargo of gasoline been aboard.

"If the Canal Commission continues on its present course, the risk of a major catastrophe will hang daily over the heads of everyone … along the route of the waterway," pilots union chief Captain James Dunworth told the *Los Angeles Times*.

The commission, of course, defended its safety record. It said it continued to inspect hazardous cargo and to conduct safety checks on vessels. It said it had improved from one major accident in 243 transits in 1980 to one in 379 in 1984. A "major accident," as the commission defined it, was one causing more than $50,000 in damage and requiring an investigation.

Canal pilot John Morales discounted the canal's safety record, saying what really mattered was the current state of repairs and upkeep. "They're playing on the canal's past safety record which is great because they used to care," he told the *Times*.

In 1987, a 450-foot-long ship with a cargo of 8,000 pounds of rice made a wrong turn in the Panama Canal into the path of another ship. The ship with rice was struck right on its main cargo hold. The collision ruptured the engine room. Nobody got killed and the other ship stayed afloat, but the ship packed with rice was wrecked beyond repair and sank to the bottom of the channel in about 30 minutes.

This accident happened about two miles ahead of me when I was piloting another ship. I came upon it and almost hit the wreckage. To avoid it, I had to go out of the channel and navigate over an underwater forest. I could hear tops of trees hit the bottom of our ship. Somehow, we made it through without any damage.

That's right, an underwater forest in the Panama Canal. When the United States created the lake, it raised the water level to 85 feet above sea level right over the existing rainforest. Everything below the water level petrified. Every tree above it in the channel, the Americans knocked down with a cable. In Gatun Lake when I dropped an anchor one time, the anchor chain got snagged and I pulled a tree straight up out of the water.

After the ship sank with its rice cargo, no one was sure at first how to get the wreckage off the bottom. Then somebody said, "Wait a minute. There's a Dutch salvage company that is working right now in South America." They called the company and, in a couple of weeks, two large salvage tugs arrived.

The salvage crew put one tug on one side of the wreck, then used divers to run a huge anchor chain under the bottom of the sunken ship to the second tug on the other side. It took them two or three days to do that while transiting ships used tugs to navigate around them. Once the anchor chain was in place, the salvage crews jerked it back and forth using a hydraulic pile and cut the ship in half. They literally sawed through the metal hull of the ship. The screeching of tearing metal was the worst sound I've ever heard. It took about three days to cut through. The crew then pulled half of the wreckage to one side of the canal and the other half to the other side.

I heard reports that the eight-day salvage operation cost over $2 million.

The only ones loving this whole mess were the fish. The rice flowed out of the sunken ship's cargo hold into the lake and gave the peacock bass a feast.

***

According to the Smithsonian, there weren't any peacock bass in Gatun Lake at all until 1969. That year, some wealthy visitors imported 60 to 100 peacock bass from Colombia to stock a pond in

Panama for sport fishing. During a rainy season, some of the fish escaped and, by the early 1970s, the peacock bass had colonized the lake. This bass (a species technically known as *Cichla monoculus*) are considered a delicious game fish, but they are also voracious predators.

A report in 1973 by scientists from the Smithsonian Tropical Research Institute field station on Barro Colorado Island in Panama discovered that the accidental release of the peacock bass had destroyed 60 percent of the native fish in Gatun Lake. A follow-up study in 2016 found almost no native fish at all.

I didn't fish much when I lived in Panama, but I was on a boat one day with a bag of marshmallows. I just happened to put one on the hook and threw it in. In no time I hooked one fish and then another. Guess what? Peacock bass love marshmallows.

After that, I would go out with a friend and say, "I bet I can catch more fish that you can." I wouldn't tell him until we started that I had a secret bait: marshmallows.

14. Russians

I boarded a Soviet cargo ship in 1983 when I was still a Step One pilot. I don't recall the ship's name, but I remember that the captain was kind of a surly fellow.

The American pilots didn't much like the Russians then. After the Soviets invaded Afghanistan a few years earlier, some pilots threatened a "sickout" so they wouldn't be forced to take Russian ships through the canal.

In 1983, President Reagan accused the U.S.S.R. of using the canal to ship arms to Nicaragua's socialist government, which was battling Contra rebels supported by the U.S. Even so, under terms of the Panama Canal treaties, the U.S. decided not to halt the ships, as the canal was supposed to remain a neutral passageway. The Soviets could go through the canal like everyone else if they paid their tolls and followed the rules and regulations.

One of those Panama Canal regulations stated that, if it was mealtime when a pilot was aboard a ship, the vessel's crew was supposed to feed him. The food wasn't always good. Sometimes the place was so dirty I didn't want to eat there anyway; I brought my own sandwich just in case. On the other hand, I was all but guaranteed a great meal on a cruise ship.

In my transit aboard the Soviet ship, we were about halfway through the canal when noontime came around. Since no one offered a meal, I spoke up.

"Captain, can I get some lunch?" I asked.

The captain responded in a thick Russian accent, "Mr. Pilot, you make a lot of money as an American. I don't feed you lunch. You get your own lunch."

I said, "Where the heck am I going to get a lunch? We're halfway across the canal."

"That's your problem. You're the pilot. You figure it out," the captain said.

As he walked away, I said, "Okay, Captain, no problem."

I got on the radio and called the Marine Traffic Control Center. I identified myself and explained that I was on this Soviet ship coming up on Gamboa and that the captain was refusing to give me lunch. I knew there was a canteen at Gamboa because I used to eat there a lot and pretty much had the menu memorized.

I requested that someone on the marine traffic staff pick up food for me in Gamboa and bring it on a launch to the Soviet ship.

The dispatcher asked, "What would you like?"

I gave him my order for two hamburgers, some fried chicken, French fries, two pizzas, a six-pack of Coca-Cola and a salad.

"Geez, are you that hungry?"

"Look, just get me what I want," I said, and I continued listing a few food items.

As we arrived at Gamboa, the ship slowed for the approaching Chagres River crossing. Along came the launch with my food. The captain was below and didn't see it arrive. His crew lowered a basket down the side of the ship to retrieve my order. They had to do this a couple of times because there was so much food.

I unpacked the food and placed it buffet-style across the open area of the bridge in front of the windows.

I turned to the Soviet crew members. "Would you guys like a piece of pizza, a hamburger or something?"

"Oh, thank you, thank you," several said as they helped themselves to the burgers, chicken and pizza. I dug into the food as well.

"Here, have a Coca-Cola," I said, handing out sodas.

We were devouring the food when the captain returned to the bridge.

"What is this?" he asked.

I said, "You told me to get my lunch. I got my lunch. Would you like some American food, Captain?"

He seemed puzzled by my kind gesture.

"You would give me some food?" he asked.

"Yeah, help yourself."

He picked up a piece of pizza. He was smiling now.

"You know, Mr. Pilot, I apologize for not giving you lunch when you ordered it. This is much nicer, though."

"Yeah, Captain, it is," I said. "And let me tell you something, just so you understand. You're paying for this."

His mouth, now full of pizza, dropped open.

I proceeded to explain that the Panama Canal would be billing the ship's owner for all the food, plus $210 for the launch to deliver it.

"You explain to your company that the reason this happened was your refusal to give me lunch. Next time you come through the canal, you remember that."

I not only got my lunch, but I taught the Soviet captain a very expensive lesson.

***

Soviet ships with questionable cargo came through the canal while I worked there. The Soviets brought ocean trawlers to Cuba and loaded them up with political dissidents who had been locked up by Cuba's communist government. The trawlers were factory ship where prisoners were forced to work. The Soviets brought these ships loaded with Cubans through the Panama Canal on ships bound for Antarctica.

I was working in the wheelhouse while taking a Soviet trawler through when the canal lockmaster called me on the radio.

He said, "Hey, Captain, stop the ship. Stop your engines."

"Why?" I asked.

He said, "We got people in the canal."

Sure enough, several of the Cubans on the trawler had put their clothes in laundry bags and jumped over the side to possibly defect to America. I looked over the ship's stern and there were about 55 to 60 of them in the locks.

I ordered the ship to stop. By then, the Cubans had climbed up the side of the locks, where they were detained by security.

Guess what the Americans did? They turned the Cubans over to Panama government officials, who put them on a bus to the pilots station, where launches were waiting. As I was leaving the Soviet ship at the end of my transit, I saw the launches transporting the Cubans back to the Soviet ship. God knows what punishment awaited them. It was very sad to see that none escaped.

***

There was another time in the mid-1980s when I had an incident with a Soviet ship.

A few days before the transit, I had installed an air conditioner in a window of my quarters. I had hired a gardener, a Panamanian-Indian fellow by the name of Sergio, who agreed to help me do the installation.

After we lifted the air conditioner into the window frame, I went outside to push it into place while he was inside holding it up. I had part of my hand inside the air conditioner when, without warning me, he plugged in the power cord. The fan went on. And immediately it almost sliced off half of my ring finger. I mean, the finger was just hanging by a thread on my left hand. Blood was all over the place. My first thought was that I was going to lose the finger.

I grabbed a towel from the clothesline and wrapped it around my hand and headed for the military hospital. God was with me: There was an Army surgeon on active duty who was a specialist in reconnecting fingers, arms and legs. He gave me a shot to relieve the pain and to kind of ease the tension. He operated, put my finger back together and saved it. It was amazing. You never could tell how bad it was by looking at that finger now.

The doctor discharged me, and I went home on medical leave. After two days, I felt pretty good and decided to go back to work.

My next assignment was on a Soviet cargo ship in Cristobal Harbor. I stepped on the pilot's ladder and began climbing up to the deck. As I attempted to climb over the ship's railing, the bandage slipped off my finger. My hand began bleeding profusely. There was blood all over my shirt. The Soviets thought I injured myself on their ship. I tried to explain otherwise, but the third officer insisted on taking me to the ship's dispensary to get patched up.

Back then, whenever Soviet ships went to sea, they carried 15 to 20 extra people. It was suspected that some were present to keep crew members from defecting. Others may have been in Soviet military intelligence.

When I arrived at the dispensary, I was introduced to the Soviet ship's doctor, a very attractive, blonde woman about 6 feet tall.

"The pilot just injured his hand on the ship," the third officer told the doctor.

"No, I didn't. I just accidentally tore the bandage off," I said.

The doctor looked at my hand.

"Sit down," she said, pointing to a gurney. "I fix your finger."

She had a Russian accent, but I was surprised she spoke pretty good English.

She cleaned my hand and did a fantastic job rebandaging my injured finger. When she finished that, she pulled out this thin rubber tubing and rolled it over my finger. It was a clever way to keep the bandage in place, but it kind of reminded me of something else, and so I started to grin mischievously.

She knew exactly why I was laughing. She took her hand and hit me upside the head and knocked me right off the gurney. I would have fallen onto the deck if the chief officer and the third mate hadn't caught me.

"You, you, you're like all other men. You're just alike," she fumed, and she walked out.

The officers took me up to the bridge where, in Russian, they told the captain what happened.

"I am so sorry. I am so sorry," the captain told me.

I said, "Captain, don't worry about it, okay? We're okay. I'm okay."

I took the ship through the canal and then to the Pacific Anchorage. The captain turned to me and said, "After we anchor, we go ashore. Would you like to go with me and my officers? We're going to a restaurant downtown. I'd like to buy you dinner."

I called the control station and said, "I won't need a car. I'm going with the Russian captain for dinner."

I got into one of two taxis loaded with Soviets and we headed for the restaurant. When we got there, guess who emerged from the other taxi? The ship's doctor.

We all went in and sat at one big table. The Russians put the doctor next to me.

"Oh, Captain," she said. "I'm sorry I hit you. I'm so sorry." I again insisted I was okay.

Over dinner, the doctor shared with me that she had been in the Soviet army until, because of some misdeed, she was banished to serve on Russian cargo ships.

"I cannot go anywhere without an escort," she said.

I told her I was so sorry to hear that.

As the meal went on, everyone at the table was drinking, except for the doctor and me. When the meal ended, the Soviet men got up and headed next door to a casino to gamble. The only ones left at the table were the doctor and me.

The others weren't gone two minutes when she leaned over and said, "Captain, Captain, I want to defect."

"What?"

The doctor repeated that she was seeking political asylum in the United States.

I said, "Hey, I can't help you. I can't get involved."

"Oh, please, please. You must help me defect," she said. "My life is over as a doctor. I must stay on these ships for the rest of my life. I got to defect."

I thought that over, then finally said, "Well, sit here a minute. I'm going to go make a phone call."

I went into the lobby of the restaurant to a pay phone and called a friend who was an Army officer working with the U.S. Embassy in Panama.

"Hey, Bob," I told him, "I got a Russian woman here," and I explained how she was aboard a Soviet ship and wanted to defect.

He said, "You tell her to be outside the restaurant in 30 minutes. Just go tell her that."

"Okay."

I went back to the table. By now several Russians, but not the captain, had returned from the casino, drinking heavily and eating again. The doctor was just sitting there.

I leaned over and whispered, "In 30 minutes, you tell them you're going to the bathroom. Instead, go out the front door. Someone will be waiting there to meet you." I looked at my watch and repeated, "30 minutes."

"Thank you very much," she said quietly.

In the meantime, the captain returned. I thanked him for the meal and left. I didn't wait around to see what happened. I got into a taxi and went back to my quarters.

The next day I got a call from a port captain.

"What happened last night?" he asked. "The doctor from the ship ran off and they can't find her. They think she's somewhere in Panama. They are going to send someone over to your quarters."

"You can send somebody if you want, but she's not with me. I don't know where she is. She didn't go with me." This was the truth, but I didn't share the full story.

After that, I never asked my Army friend about the Russian doctor, and he never spoke about it, either. To this day I don't know what happened to her, but I'd like to think she went on to a happy life.

15. Salaries and bonuses

WHEN I was hired as a Panama Canal pilot, our wages were marginal compared with the rest of the maritime industry. My initial salary was about $45,000 a year as an apprentice; then, it increased to $65,000 when I became a Step One pilot. It increased periodically after that at each step level. That might seem extraordinarily good for the early 1980s when the minimum wage was $3.35 an hour and the average salary in the United States was $15,000 a year. But in those days, captains were making about $105,000 to $110,000 a year on general American cargo ships, and mates were making $85,000.

After the apprenticeship was completed, my work rotation became six weeks of working on the canal followed by four weeks off. Those six weeks were always quite demanding: I was on call every day, with the only limitation being that I had to receive at least 16 hours off following a transit.

We had a union hall where the pilots gathered when they weren't on duty. I'd hear them often complain that they deserved bigger salaries. I used to tick some of them off by saying, "Guys, why did you come here? You knew what the money was." One time, I was even thrown out of the union hall while the pilots were in contract negotiations with the commission. One pilot said to me, "You're a lousy negotiator. You can't negotiate because the company knows you love your job. Go back to work taking ships through the canal."

The truth was, I did love my job, right from the beginning.

First and foremost, apprentices were fortunate to receive any kind of salary. Elsewhere in the world, apprentice pilots rarely got paid until they were certified, licensed working pilots. And it could take him three, five or even 10 years to get necessary licenses and certifications before he was accepted for a job, with no pay in the meantime. If that had been in the case in Panama, I couldn't have afforded to train there.

Becoming a pilot in most places in the 1980s, as today, was very demanding, time-consuming and economically costly. Those higher salaries later would help offset the loss of income while in the training phase for a specific harbor. For example, in New York Harbor, it can take a licensed mariner up to 12 years to qualify. Then, to get a job, it still depends on the availability of an opening.

Piloting on the Panama Canal was a U.S. civil service job. We did not have to pay for our training, our retirement or our medical insurance. We also received government-subsidized housing, which is why my initial rent for a home was just $400 a month.

As the treaties took effect, some of the perks disappeared. Many Americans had to move out of the assigned housing as the former Canal Zone became integrated to Panamanians.

The U.S. government also closed its civilian commissary in 1984. Americans now had to shop in downtown Panama City. The quality of food, the selection and the prices weren't as good as what Americans had received at the commissary.

Because Panama Canal employees lost their commissary privileges, the commission decided to compensate them with free housing. Incredibly, the commission stated that canal pilots and other commission personnel who were ex-military had to still pay rent because we could shop at the local Army commissary. Those of us who were veterans didn't think that was fair. We had earned commissary and PX benefits through years of military service, often at risk to our lives. We didn't think these benefits should cancel our right to another.

About nine of us, including a retired four-star Navy captain, filed a grievance against the Panama Canal Commission. Eventually, we won. The U.S. Army comptroller directed the commission to refund to us about three years of rent.

Over my 16 years in Panama, there was constant turmoil between the pilots union and the commission. The union was always seeking more money and more benefits, which is what unions do. If there was a way to squeeze a few extra dollars out of the commission, the pilots would try to do it.

The union eventually succeeded in negotiating several bonus systems that paid pilots extra for doing additional work.

One system rewarded a pilot for taking additional ships through the canal. In a two-week period, a pilot was asked to take a minimum of seven ships. If he did eight ships, he got a bonus equal to four hours of pay. For nine or ten ships, the bonus was eight hours of pay for each ship. If he took eleven or more ships through during that two-week period – which was really pushing it – he got a bonus of sixteen hours of pay.

There was also a bonus system for Panama Canal pilots working the harbors. Every time we worked harbor duty, we received a bonus for moving a ship.

These bonus systems could really pump up our paychecks.

At the same time, many of the Americans working on the canal tried to get out of paying U.S. income taxes. A sentence in the Revised Panama Canal Treaties stated that "United States citizen employees and dependents shall be exempt on any taxes, fees or other charges on income received as a result of their work for the commission."

The attorneys for the IRS claimed that the treaty only meant to protect the workers from having to pay Panamanian taxes – not to avoid paying those owed to the U.S. They blamed a typographical error, saying the word "Panamanian" had accidentally been left out between the words "any" and "taxes."

Several pilots and other canal employees filed federal lawsuits against the government over this tax issue. I joined one of the suits, putting up $200 toward the cost of hiring a tax lawyer to argue our case. Our main contention was that the wording in the treaty was no accident; the commission lured pilots to Panama and kept others working there by making sure the treaties promised the workers wouldn't have to pay income taxes. In other words, exemption from income taxes was the U.S. government's carrot to retain employees.

I knew we were making an argument in a gray area, which is why I continued to pay my taxes. However, several others stopped paying their taxes. It turned out to be a very foolish move on their part.

The U.S. Supreme Court ruled unanimously in 1986 that Americans working in Panama had to pay their U.S. taxes. By then, some pilots and others owed for eight years of back taxes. For some, it amounted to a quarter of a million dollars. One Panama Canal pilot told reporters that the IRS began garnishing nearly 98 percent of his bimonthly paycheck, leaving him with about $150 per pay period.

16. Nautical school

EVERY time I had four weeks off from piloting duties, I flew home to Washington State to spend time with my family and to teach at Vancouver Marine Consultants, a nautical school I started in 1980. By 1984, the school had helped more than 400 people in the Seattle-Portland area get their captain's licenses. I was quoted in *The Spillway*, a newsletter for canal employees, saying: "Someday, I'm going to have the best nautical school in the United States."

I designed classes to teach young men and women the basic skills to enter the lower ranks as seamen and to seek jobs on small craft along U.S. rivers and coastlines. I also provided U.S. Coast Guard licensing preparatory classes for tug masters, including seminars in safety, fire-fighting and marine first aid aboard vessels in the Pacific Northwest. I would sometimes board the vessels for days at a time, supervising crews through repeated drills until they mastered the techniques.

I enjoyed sharing the lessons I had learned from nearly 25 years in the maritime industry.

"I can feed back into the system some of the advice I received when I was young and needed help," I told *The Spillway*.

My wife set up the class schedule while I was piloting on the canal. Then, I'd get off the airplane from Panama and, two days later, I'd be teaching a class.

The classes ran 8 a.m. to 5 p.m. daily for two weeks. Every morning Shirley was there to make coffee for the students. They were all young men. One was a gentleman – I'll call him Charlie – who worked as a towboat seaman in Seattle. Charlie is British, and so my wife, whose parents were born in England, offered to make tea especially for him. They hit it off right away, and during our 10 o'clock break, they often went outside to have a cup of tea and smoke a cigarette.

On the third day of classes, Charlie showed up with a bouquet of flowers. He gave them to Shirley and said to me, "I just love your wife. She's just so nice." And from then on, he brought her a bouquet of flowers every morning.

In the evening Shirley would tell me, "What a nice man Charlie is. He always brings me flowers. Why can't you bring me flowers once in a while?"

This went on for two weeks until Charlie graduated from the course. He got his captain's license, and he went back to Seattle.

A couple of days later, while sitting with the family eating dinner. Shirley said, "If Charlie were here right now, we'd have flowers on the table."

Now I can't remember who told me, but someone had just shared the source of the flowers. Next to the motel where Charlie was staying was a cemetery, and every morning Charlie went there and took a bouquet from one of the graves to bring to Shirley.

When Shirley brought up the flowers over dinner, I told the story and said to her, "Well, I guess if you want flowers, I know where I can get them." She got up from the table and left without a word, but later she would laugh about the strange gift of cemetery flowers.

I ran into Charlie several years later at a conference. When I brought up that we found out about the flowers, he just laughed.

"Where else was I going to get flowers so early in the morning?" he said.

By 1984, my time away in Panama and the stresses of the commute had put additional strain on our marriage. Shirley and I decided to separate. We divorced the following year.

Shirley continued to operate the nautical school, bringing in friends of mine to teach. The school continued to operate until the 1990s.

17. Living in Panama

WHEN I began training in Panama, after a period living in a hotel, I moved to government housing in Margarita on the Atlantic side of the canal. Most pilots didn't like living there or in nearby Cristobal because of the mosquito and termite infestations as well as other creatures. There literally were bats in the belfry of my building.

The traditional housing situation for American canal workers was based strictly on seniority. When someone left Panama or vacated a set of quarters for a nicer set, the employee next highest on the housing list was given priority to move in.

After I became a Step One pilot, to my surprise, a clerk informed me that the commission was giving new pilots five years' worth of housing seniority.

"Look at any house you want," she said. "There are twelve here in Balboa, four in Curundu and seven in the Ancon area. You don't have to live in Margarita anymore."

I managed to land a nice two-story apartment in Balboa. Later I learned that this kind bump in housing seniority did not go over very well with longtime employees who had waited for years on that list.

During my time off, I liked to explore downtown Panama City, visit shops, and just walk up and down the streets. The restaurants were fabulous and the menus reasonably priced. Some of the best pizzas in the world are served in Panama.

Panama is also a wonderful place for those interested in history, architecture and nature. The area is peppered with Spanish colonial buildings, 400-year-old forts, parks, small shops selling authentic native goods, rainforests crawling with exotic creatures, and some of the best fishing spots in the world.

Every Saturday, you could just show up at strangers' weddings in Panama's beautiful old churches. The ceremonies were always very colorful. It was not unusual at the end of the ceremony for a priest or usher to pass a collection plate. Of course, you were expected to add a few dollars for the privilege of watching the wedding.

***

Wednesdays when I wasn't working on the canal, I would often gather for coffee at the Elks Club Balboa with a group that included a priest, a rabbi, a Baptist minister and a Mormon. I loved to hear them swap stories about their places of worship.

One day the priest mentioned he had a parishioner – an older lady named Miss Marie – who came to his Mass every morning. The Baptist minister said, "Oh, I know her. She comes to my church Sundays and for Wednesday night prayer meetings." And another minister said she came to all his services – what's more, he said, each time the collection plate was passed, she managed to slip out a little for herself. The others piped up and said, "That's what she does at my church, too!"

None seemed to mind that Miss Marie was sustaining herself off their cash flow. In Panama, there were all kinds of ways people made money, and you learned to accept it.

Complaining one day that my tooth was hurting, a Panamanian pilot suggested I go see his brother, who was a dentist. I immediately got in my car and drove downtown to the brother's dental clinic. After a brief exam, he informed me I needed four root canals. As he worked away, I nervously leaned back and let him do his thing. I was impressed at how experienced he seemed until his wife came in and started chatting. I don't think she was aware I understood when she said in Spanish, "Oh, I see you're doing your first root canal." Nonetheless, he seemed to know what he was doing.

Finally, the procedure ended, and I was relieved until he told me I needed to come back three more times. He had only done one root canal.

I said, "Just do them all at once."

"But then I can't charge you four times as much," he said.

In Panama, one of the most unique money-making schemes involved "red devil" buses. Entrepreneurs bought up these rickety school buses in Miami and had them shipped to Panama. They'd fix them a little, repaint them with artwork, including murals of girlfriends, athletes or communist figures. Then they'd run independent routes throughout Panama. The owners paid the city a small daily fee for a permit to run the buses wherever they wanted. For passengers, the only way you'd know where the bus was stopping was to ask the driver when you got on. In recent years, the government has been trying to shut down these buses, which are known for their reckless drivers and deadly crashes.

***

In the first few years I worked on the canal, I felt relatively safe in Panama City. However, even then, I would never go downtown late at night. There was a lot of poverty, not to mention lingering anti-American sentiment. If you were downtown at 2 o'clock in the morning, it was all but guaranteed you're going to get robbed or worse.

Things got dicier under the dictatorship of General Manuel Noriega, who came into power after Panamanian leader Omar Torrijos – the president of Panama who signed the treaties with the U.S. – was killed in a mysterious plane crash in July 1981.

Under Noriega, the police became just as corrupt as the criminals. Panama outside the former Canal Zone became a dangerous, dangerous place. The police under Noriega generally were smart enough not to bother Americans when they were occupying a Panama Canal vehicle. But if you were a private citizen in your own car and you drove out of the canal area, you were fair game. Police would pull people over and give the driver tickets for anything and everything, then demand a bribe. It was not unusual to be stopped on a street corner by a Panamanian Guardia demanding you give him $10 or $20.

I had bars on my apartment windows and double locks on the doors. Criminals would still break in. It got to the point that when I returned to the States for four weeks, I'd leave my TV set and air conditioner right inside the front door. That way, when they broke in, they'd take them and usually wouldn't look for anything more. Even then, occasionally, they would steal other goods, from a rice cooker to shaving cream.

Many of the Americans working in Panama sent their families home because it got so dangerous. Those married to Panamanians generally were okay, especially if they spoke fluent Spanish. They could negotiate their way out of difficulties.

As Noriega became more and more powerful – and the U.S. government ignored his drug-running – he became a figure of almost mythic reputation.

On one of my return flights to Panama, I learned the passenger next to me, Corky Steiner, was from Cincinnati, just down the river from where I grew up. We got chatting, and Corky mentioned he was vice president of operations in Central America for Kenner Toys, which his father owned. I invited him to join me on a transit of the canal.

When Corky was in Panama, he stayed downtown at the Holiday Inn. From his room, he could look down into a beautiful residence. From his description, I knew what he saw: Noriega's compound. When I told him that, Corky insisted he wanted to tour the place, apparently to discuss a business deal.

"You don't want to do that," I said.

Corky said, "Don't worry about it. I speak fluent Spanish."

Sure enough, the next day he knocked on the door of the compound and Noriega's security people welcomed him inside. If he made a business deal, I never heard about it.

I do know this: Within a year of learning that several other Panama Canal pilots and I supported a children's hospital and burn center in Panama, Corky shipped a huge container of Kenner toys as gifts for the kids.

To this day, he and I remain good friends.

***

In Panama in the 1980s, there always seemed to be a party at somebody's place. One time I was setting up a dinner party at my apartment with the help of my maid and a neighbor, a female teacher. We heard a loud bang on the corrugated roof over the top of my patio. I went outside and saw a bullet hole in the roof. On the concrete floor was a smashed .45-caliber round. It was clear to me someone nearby fired a gun in the air, the bullet went up, and then it came down through my roof. Fortunately, no one was standing under it.

Without telling me first, the maid called the Panamanian police. The Guardia had a station right around the corner. When they showed up, a sergeant said to me, "Did anybody get hurt?"

"No," I told him.

"What happened?"

I explained that someone I didn't know must have fired a gun upward and the bullet happened to come down at my place.

One of the Guardia then asked me, "Are you and your girlfriend having problems?" It seemed a stupid question, so I impulsively gave a sarcastic answer.

"That's right. I wanted to shoot her. So, I went out on the patio and shot a gun in the air," I said.

In seconds, the Guardia had me in handcuffs. The cops immediately took me to the police station and began an interrogation.

"Were you trying to shoot your neighbor girlfriend?" a detective asked.

"No, I wasn't," I said. "I was joking with this officer, trying to explain that somebody fired a gun into the air. The bullet went up and had to come down. I am an ex-military marksman. A bullet that goes up travels 32 feet per second and then comes down at the same speed minus wind resistance. Do you know how accurate I'd have to be to do something like that to shoot her?"

It took four hours before they released me. I ended up paying a $20 fine.

Life in Panama was getting more dangerous by the day.

18. A pooping monkey and killer bees

I was piloting a Chinese cargo ship, heading north across the canal, when the young captain asked if it was all right if his wife came to the bridge.

"Well, Captain," I said, "it's your ship. Of course, she can come to the bridge."

The wife soon arrived and stood quietly on one side of the pilothouse. She carried a large purse that looked a bit like a laundry bag.

Everything seemed fine, nothing unusual. But then I looked over and saw her putting something into the bag. And the bag was moving. I finally determined she had food in her hand and she was feeding something.

Suddenly, the bag popped open and out jumped this creature – a tiny spider monkey. It looked terribly frightened. The animal immediately started going crazy, jumping on everything, while the crew tried to catch it.

It was all kind of amusing until the monkey got so excited it began to poop. Not just little poop jobs, either. Out came something resembling an aerosol spray. The poop flew everywhere, on everything, and it smelled as bad as the water buffalo.

While this was occurring, I continued giving navigational orders as we entered the Gaillard Cut. Here we were, passing other ships nearby while ducking the monkey and dodging its poop. This went on for so long that I began to think to myself: That monkey has got to die. No animal can possibly lose that much body secretion and still live.

I shouted to no one in particular, "For heaven's sake, catch that gosh-darn monkey," or words to that effect.

The captain yelled back, "I'll get a gun! I'll shoot the monkey!"

I was certain he was serious. On most commercial ships, all captains have a gun in their safe to protect themselves and valuables.

"No, no, you don't shoot the monkey," I said. "Catch the monkey."

After several tries, the crew finally trapped the creature inside a trash can. They put a top on the can and then took the monkey off the bridge. The wife disappeared, and I never saw her again.

By now, I was standing outside because the wheelhouse smelled so bad. For the next two hours, as we went across Gatun Lake to the anchorage area, the crew cleaned the pilot house the best they could, but it was almost impossible to get rid of the odor.

The captain was especially embarrassed, of course. When we completed the transit, arriving in Cristobal Harbor, I said to the captain, "The ship is yours." He thanked me very much and apologized profusely. He offered me a bottle of whiskey. At that time, commercial ship captains carried what is known as a "slop chest," a supply of whiskey and cigarettes and items they could trade for favors in some ports.

I politely declined his offer of whiskey.

As I climbed down the pilot's ladder to the launch, one of the ship's crew members lowered a bag down to me. I thought, well, I guess he didn't want me to leave without a gift. The launch seaman took the bag and said, "Here, Captain."

Just as I was reaching for the bag, it moved. I didn't have to look inside to know that the captain had foisted the monkey off on me.

"No," I shouted back up to the crew, "I don't want the monkey."

And the mate on the deck said, "The captain said that you take the monkey. Please, you take the monkey."

So, I took the monkey.

When I tell this story, people always want to know what happened to my pooping monkey. I explain that I didn't keep it. I tell them I carefully transported the animal back with me to shore. In the jitney on my way across the isthmus, I rolled down a window and let it loose in the jungles of Panama. I'm certain it lived happily ever after. To this day, if you're ever transiting the Panama Canal and you see two beady eyes staring at you from the nearby jungle, it just might be my monkey, or perhaps even one of its babies.

After this incident, I tell people, I've never looked at monkeys the same way again. I don't even go to the zoo anymore.

That's my monkey story. I swear it's absolutely true. You can't make up stories like this.

***

Here's another one about wildlife and me:

I brought a large tanker – a dry bulk carrier, which just had nothing but flat decks – through the canal. We were just getting into the Cut, and going pretty slow, when I looked up on the bow and saw crewmen and linemen jumping overboard. There were about 15 or 20 of them leaping right into the Gaillard Cut. Fortunately, the bow was close to the water line, so they only had to drop 15 or 20 feet to reach the water.

I next saw one of the ship's officers running back toward the bridge with a walkie-talkie, looking like he was trying to find a place to hide.

I said, "Oh, my God. What the heck is happening up there?"

"Killer bees!" someone shouted. "It's a swarm of killer bees!"

By then I had heard about the Africanized killer bees migrating from South America. They were first spotted in Panama near the Colombian border in February 1982. But this was the first time I had seen them crossing the canal as they headed north.

The bees, which originated in Africa, were released by accident in Brazil in the late 1950s while they were being studied for research. The bees were known for their superior production of honey as well as their aggressive nature. According to news reports at the time, a peasant in Panama ended up in the hospital after he was repeatedly stung while trying to hack into an African bee hive.

When these bees attacked us, we halted the ship to retrieve the men from the canal, transferred them to medical care and sought replacement line handlers. No one was seriously injured from the stings or from jumping overboard.

I spent 2½ years in Vietnam and I lived in other countries with all sorts of insects. But I never saw anything as nasty as these killer bees.

A happier memory of insects during my years as a Panama Canal pilot was the seasonal migration of monarch butterflies. Every spring, huge clouds of these colorful butterflies crossed Panama fluttering their way toward North America.

19. Chinese interpreter

PILOTING a Chinese ship in the 1980s was unlike any other. The communist Chinese then were getting back into the Merchant Marine industry and adding container ships. Because they were new to modern shipping, the Chinese often turned to experienced mariners from democratic Taiwan to work as officers overseeing the communist Chinese crew. The two didn't get along politically; but like two brothers who fight, you didn't want to get between them.

The Chinese crews these days speak English very well. But in the 1980s, on a lot of Chinese ships coming through, the crews didn't speak English, even though English is the standard language of the sea. With Chinese ships, there was both a language and cultural barrier that often led to misunderstandings with the American pilots.

One morning about 5 o'clock, I was aboard a Chinese ship with three other pilots having a cup of coffee before we got underway. One of the pilots out of the blue turned to another pilot and said, "Are you Jewish?"

"Yeah, I'm Jewish. So what?"

The first pilot said, "I was thinking, I've been all over the world. I was wondering, are there Jews in China?"

And another pilot said, "Sure, there are Jews in China."

"No, no, no. You don't understand what I'm talking about. Are there any Chinese who are Jewish?"

"Well, heck, I don't know," the Jewish pilot said. "Let's find out."

The two of them went over to the Chinese captain, who could barely speak English, and they repeated this inane question.

"Are there are Jews in China?"

The captain said, "I don't know what you mean. You should talk to the chief officer. He speaks good English."

After the chief officer came over, they asked him, "Are there any Chinese Jews?"

He got a befuddled look on his face. Finally, he said, "No, but we have orange juice, tomato juice, pineapple juice, but no Chinese juice."

I don't think we stopped laughing the entire transit.

***

Often when pilots took a foreign ship through, especially ones from countries where few spoke English as a second language, we were provided an interpreter from Panama.

The pilots generally didn't like interpreters. After one Chinese interpreter did a transit with us a couple of times, he began to act like he was the pilot and started giving orders on his own. It could become unnerving when the rudder was sent in the wrong direction because the interpreter gave the wrong order. When there was an interpreter on board, you had to pay special attention to the orders regarding engine positions, controls and rudders.

In the mid-1980s, I was the solo pilot on a Chinese cargo ship. That's where I first met an interpreter by the name of Mr. Cho. He claimed he had been an interpreter as a young man for the Chinese leader Chiang Kai-shek during World War II. Of course, Mr. Cho spoke very good English.

I worked well with him, and we became friends. Eventually, he invited me to tour the buildings where the Chinese lived and worked in Panama. These included businesses in Cristobal where they had gambling saloons in the basements, which had been connected from building to building so they could go from one to another undetected.

Mr. Cho also gave me some interesting history of the Chinese in Panama, explaining how many of them had died from malaria and yellow fever after arriving as construction workers. Some committed suicide to avoid a lingering death during the 1850s construction of the Panama railway linking the Atlantic with the Pacific. Afterward, those who survived helped to launch vast immigration of Chinese into Panamanian life.

Mr. Cho ran a language school in Panama for the Chinese who were flocking to Panama during the 1980s. After Noriega took over Panama, about 35,000 to 40,000 Chinese paid upward of $10,000 each to the government for instant Panamanian citizenship. Many then used this citizenship to obtain a U.S. visa within a year or two. The corruption at that time was amazing.

When he found out I was ex-military, Mr. Cho asked me if I could obtain a pair of American Army military shoes for him. He just liked Army shoes. I got him a pair, size 8 regular, black.

Not long afterward he called me to ask if I would like to go to dinner. I accepted and looked forward to it. When I arrived at a restaurant in Panama City, he was sitting at the table across from a very attractive young Chinese woman. She couldn't speak a word of English or Spanish. But she sat there very prim and proper. Eventually, she excused herself to go to the ladies room.

Mr. Cho leaned close to me and very quietly asked, "Captain, what do you think?"

"What do I think about what?"

"What do you think about the girl?"

I said, "She very nice."

"Just nice?"

"Yeah, she's nice. I don't know her, but she seems nice."

We finished dinner, and nothing more was said about our female guest.

About a week later, Mr. Cho invited me to dinner once more. I got to the restaurant, and this time there was a different young Chinese woman who also couldn't speak English. When she excused herself during the meal, Mr. Cho asked me what I thought of her, and again I said our dinner companion seemed nice.

After the third time this happened, I mentioned these dinners to a Panamanian fellow who knew Mr. Cho well. He began to laugh and said, "He's a matchmaker. He's trying to fix you up with one of these Chinese girls. He wants to know if you want one."

I was taken aback. "I don't want a Chinese girl."

"Then you better stop going out with Cho for dinner, because sooner or later he's going to leave one with you."

The next time he called, I said, "No more dinner, Mr. Cho. No more matchmaking. Find somebody else."

"Okay," he said. "But I get another pair of shoes?"

I said, "Yeah, I'll get you another pair of shoes. But no more Chinese matchmaking."

Mr. Cho was a nice man, but what a character.

20. Queen Elizabeth II

ONE transit I always enjoyed as a pilot was working aboard the Queen Elizabeth II, a 964-foot luxury cruise ship built for the Cunard Line. It was a huge ship for its time, with a crew of about 1,000 and enough berths for more than 1,800 passengers. By the time I made my third transit on the QE2, I knew the captain well because he had taken the ship through previously.

"Ken, good to have you," he said. "I'm going to assign a cabin steward for you and the other pilot. If you want something to drink, you want coffee, you want something to eat, he'll take care of you. He'll be your serf for the day."

Before long the steward, a young kid who spoke broken English, came over and said, "Oh, Pilot. I am so excited. This is my first trip through the canal. I've never been a steward for a pilot."

The ship's captain, right, and I pose on the deck of the Queen Elizabeth II during a transit of the Panama Canal in 1987.

A light bulb went off. Ever since I was in the Navy, I liked to devil those who worked for me. As a pilot, I looked for similar openings where I could have a little fun or lighten the mood with crews when it wouldn't interfere with operations.

I gave the steward a stern look.

"You may be my steward," I said, "but you better get my breakfast correct or I'm going to throw your butt overboard."

"I get it right."

I said, "You better get it right." I looked over at the captain and winked.

The captain piped up. "That's right. If he goes over the side, I'll get another one. I got a lot of stewards down below."

The steward then asked me, "What do you want, Pilot?"

I said, "I'll tell you what I want. I want two pieces of rye toast, lightly buttered. I want black coffee, a glass of orange juice, two bangers (that's what the British call sausage) and two eggs, one sunny-side-up and one turned over."

He looked at me, apparently committing it to memory.

I said, "Write it down."

So, he wrote it down. Then I made him read it back to me before he scurried off.

A half-hour later he came back with a tray with my breakfast. He placed it on the pilot's table on the bridge, and he then put my breakfast out.

He seemed pleased he got the order just the way I wanted it until I literally grabbed him by the back of the belt.

"You're going over the side. You screwed up my breakfast," I said.

He got a panicked look. "How did I screw up your breakfast?"

"You turned the wrong egg over."

21. India Star

I was aboard a ship that was delayed in the locks. I walked out on the bridge wing and happened to look at the ship in the adjacent lock. I recognized it as the India Star. I could see the captain wandering the bridge. I knew Omar because he came through the canal quite a bit. He was a very nice man but always a little bit nervous about his container ship bumping around in the canal.

I called him on the ship-to-ship radio.

"India Star, India Star. This is your agent."

Of course, I wasn't his agent. An agent is a person hired by a shipping company to manage the ship's needs in a port, including paperwork, supplies, mail delivery, transit fees and any miscellaneous shore side support. Omar had no idea the guy calling his radio was yours truly on the ship next to him.

"Yes, sir, Mr. Agent, what can I do for you?" he responded.

I said, "Captain, I just got word from the Panama Canal Commission that you haven't paid your tolls."

"That is unlikely. I always pay my tolls. My company pays my tolls before we go through. My tolls are paid."

I tried to sound a little impatient.

"Captain, look. I'm just your agent. They told me your tolls have not been paid. If you get out in that lake and haven't paid, they're going to have to turn you around and take you back."

Omar said, "I've never heard of anything like this in my life. I will call my company."

I said, "Captain, I'm sorry. I'm just the agent."

By now, I could see him jumping around on the bridge. He was going squirrelly.

So, I said, "Captain let me check with the canal and look into this."

Five minutes later, I called back.

"India Star, India Star. This is your agent."

"Yes, Mr. Agent, did you check with the authorities?"

I said, "Yes, Captain, and I think we have a solution. The Panama Canal authorities have noticed you have women on board."

Omar, like many of the captains who hailed from India, stayed at sea for two or three years at a time, so his shipping company allowed his family to live aboard with him.

"Yes, I have two women on board – my wife and my daughter. What has that to do with anything?" he asked me.

I said, "The authorities have told me that, if you leave one of these women ashore, you can proceed on your transit. When the tolls are paid, we'll see she is shipped up to you. We'll just keep her here in the meantime to make sure the tolls are paid."

"I never heard of anything like this in my life. This is crazy. This is crazy. What am I going to do?"

I said, "You either give us one of those women, pay your tolls, or we're going to turn you around."

By now, Omar is going absolutely crazy. I'm sure he was contemplating the thousands of dollars his shipping company would lose if he were delayed going through the canal.

Finally, he said, "Which one should I pick?" referring to his wife and his daughter.

"I don't care," I said. "But you need to leave one of them ashore."

I let that sink in for a minute or so before picking up the radio again.

"India Star, India Star. Look over on your starboard side."

"What's that got to do with anything?"

I said, "Just look over there."

Then I stepped out of the wheelhouse and waved. I said, "Omar, it's me, Kenny. You can proceed."

Fortunately, I saw him smile.

"Oh, Kenny, if I get a hold of you, I'll kill you. You make me crazy."

The devil made me do it.

22. Blind pilot

WE always had a few ship captains who went out of their way to give Panama Canal pilots a hard time. There was an especially arrogant one on a Japanese container ship. He repeatedly messed with our pilots, for whatever reason. If a pilot said, "Port 10 degrees rudder," he'd set it as Port 15. And he would repeat our orders in Japanese, even though conversations were supposed to be in English. This went on for numerous transits until some of the pilots got fed up and someone said, "This guy needs to be straightened out." Guess I was getting a reputation as a bit of a prankster.

I requested and was assigned to be the control pilot the next time that Japanese ship was scheduled to transit the canal. When that day came, I boarded the ship while wearing dark, wrap-around sunglasses. I carefully climbed the pilot's ladder, moving my hands like I was feeling my way. When I arrived on deck, I unfolded a white cane.

A Japanese officer met me at the ladder. He looked at me and said, "Excuse me, please, who are you?"

I said, "I'm your pilot."

"You're who?"

"I'm your *anjin* (the Japanese word for ship pilot). Take me to the bridge."

"You can't see?"

I said, "No. I'm blind. Please help me to the bridge."

The officer grabbed his radio. I heard him talking to the bridge in Japanese. By now the captain could see me tapping the deck with the white cane as I walked toward him. When I arrived on the bridge, I began to bump into things.

The captain came over.

"Excuse me, please, who are you?"

I turned around, reaching out my arm as if trying to find his hand to shake.

"I'm your pilot," I said.

"What's the matter with your eyes?"

I said, "I'm blind. I was on a Japanese ship yesterday and fell down and hit my head and now I'm temporarily blind. The good news, Captain, if I take one more ship through the canal, I can retire. So, I'm taking your ship through."

The captain shook his head. "You can't take my ship."

I said, "I'm sorry, Captain, it's either me or you don't go."

"You don't take my ship. You're crazy. You're crazy."

"I'm not crazy," I said. "I don't need to see, Captain. I have the canal memorized. I can take you through the canal."

"You're crazy. I'm not going through with a blind pilot."

The second control pilot, Captain Dwight Osborne, had come aboard and joined me. As the first control pilot, I was assigned to take the ship halfway through the canal, then he would take over. I could see Dwight standing to the side of the wheelhouse. He didn't want anything to do with my stunt. He just shook his head.

Right about then I picked up a hot towel from a supply provided to pilots to clean their hands after they climbed that dirty pilot's ladder. I put the towel over my eyes for an instant. Then I took it off and looked around.

"Captain Osborne, it's a miracle! I can see! I can see!"

That's about the time the captain realized I was pulling his chain. In a quick motion, he angrily tossed his walkie-talkie radio across the wheelhouse and right through the door like he was the NFL's Johnny Unitas tossing a pass. The $1,000 radio went right over the side of the ship and into the water.

"I'm leaving the bridge. You've got the ship, Pilot" he said, and he stormed off.

For the next eight hours, Dwight and I quietly took the ship through the canal without further incident. No one said anything further about my little prank.

When we reached the other end, I said to the chief officer, "Get the captain back up here."

He didn't want to do it, but I insisted that we had to turn control of the ship back over to the captain in person. Before long, the captain showed up on the bridge, and this time he was smiling.

He came right over to me and said, "You're a very funny man. You made me crazy, but you're a funny man. You're a funny pilot. I have brought this ship through the canal many times, but I never had this happen."

I said, "That's right. And by the way, quit giving pilots a hard time."

"Oh, no more. No more. I learned my lesson."

I don't recall having any further issues with this captain.

23. Don't ask, don't tell

WHEN I became a senior pilot, I took several U.S. Navy vessels, including a few nuclear submarines, through the canal. I volunteered for these assignments, and spent time training to do so, because a lot of other pilots didn't like to work with the military ships and because I enjoyed renewing the connection.

Even in the 1980s, there were hard feelings among some pilots who had come through the Merchant Marine system due to the way they were treated after World War II. Merchant mariners had played a big role in winning the war by serving on some of the 19,000 ships that carried personnel, supplies and equipment for U.S. forces. About 8,200 mariners were killed during World War II, while hundreds of thousands of others risked their lives.

However, when the war ended, all mariners were denied federal veterans benefits, including healthcare, educational aid and disability compensation. The attitude of American leadership at the time was that the Merchant Marine guys made a lot of money during the war and they didn't need the same benefits as the military guys.

Finally, in the late 1970s and into the mid-1980s, the U.S. government began to fully recognize the mariners' wartime sacrifices and authorized giving them comparable veterans benefits. However, by then a lot of them were dead.

Besides this benefits issue, some pilots on the Panama Canal simply didn't like military people. Perhaps this attitude developed during training when they were students at the U.S. Merchant Marine Academy in King's Point, New York. It's a paramilitary school, and the

An aerial port bow view of the destroyer USS Arthur W. Radford (DD-968) navigating the Panama Canal on June 1, 1980. (Photo from the U.S. National Archives.)

discipline was as tough as anywhere in the military. Graduates received reserve officer commissions in the U.S. Navy. However, most ended up in civilian jobs on ships.

To be honest, a lot of military ship officers didn't enjoy working with pilots, either. Navy captains usually were nervous wrecks going through the canal because they didn't like relinquishing complete navigational control of their ship to a civilian pilot. While a pilot could get away with having an accident, such was not the case for the captain of a U.S. military ship. If a Navy captain had an accident, he automatically lost his command. It didn't matter whether it was his fault or not. There's no freedom to fail in the U.S. Navy, whereas owners of merchant ships usually don't fire the captain unless he's proven to be negligent.

Fortunately, there were a handful of us ex-military guys who always volunteered to take the Navy vessels. We sympathized with the pressure on these captains for a safe transit.

I think I took four submarines through the canal over the years, including the USS Ohio. Each time, the submarine was coming from the Atlantic side after departing the shipyard in Groton, Connecticut, and making shakedown cruises.

I found that nuclear submarines didn't handle like ships that float on the water. Subs were difficult to navigate because of their hull design. Some had auxiliary power thrust propeller units that extend and retract from the hull to assist in maneuvering. They also were very difficult to steer in shallow water. They could get near the bank of the canal, pick up suction and lose steering control. Piloting them was a very tenuous, mind-exhausting process that really took a lot of concentration.

Most of the time, it was just the pilot and the captain in the conning tower. It was extremely hot there, and lunch usually consisted of only a sandwich. "You don't get extra pay for it, so why do it?" one pilot told me about submarine transits and the higher risk of an accident. "If I don't have to, why take the chance?"

***

Despite my service in the Army and Navy, I was not immune to confrontations with officers aboard military ships. One time, I was a harbor pilot assigned to a Navy destroyer that seemed to show up out of nowhere. After I boarded, I met with the captain and an admiral, who was apparently on board to supervise a special project.

I soon learned the ship had to be put to anchor because the Navy had not paid the tolls.

"Admiral and Captain, I'm sorry," I said. "The U.S. Navy did not transfer the funds into our coffers. You're not going through the canal until the toll situation is worked out."

We went back and forth on this a bit until the admiral out of frustration demanded to know if I knew anything about the way the Navy worked.

"Were you in the military?" he yelled.

"No," I lied, "I was never in the military. I'm a civilian."

I wasn't taking the chance he had enough pull to throw me back into uniform.

Within a day, the Navy settled the tolls. The ship completed its transit.

***

I was assigned to be the harbor pilot to undock a Navy tanker that had brought fuel to a military base in Panama. The commander was a guy who liked to give pilots a hard time and was just generally uncooperative. None of the other pilots, even the ex-military guys, wanted to work with him.

Before I arrived at the tanker for that assignment, I borrowed a blonde wig from one of my friends who was a nurse. I put on lipstick and began walking down the pier toward the ship. This was 1994, when President Bill Clinton's administration had just initiated the "Don't Ask, Don't Tell" policy prohibiting the U.S. military from harassing or discriminating against closeted gays or bisexuals.

The crew on the tanker went crazy when they saw me coming. The sailors didn't know who I was, or what I was trying to do; I was unlike anything they had seen before on a Navy ship.

I walked up the gangway and said, "Good morning, Lieutenant. I'm your pilot. I'm going to take you to sea."

The lieutenant said, "Well, you better not go up to the bridge dressed like that."

I said, "I'll dress any way I want. I'm a pilot. What are you talking about? You take me to the bridge." On the way up, I could hear the sailors just cracking up.

The captain came into the wheelhouse and, when he saw me, let loose with a few four-letter superlatives.

"What's with the lipstick and hair?" he asked.

I said, "Captain, I just came out. Isn't this one of those don't-ask, don't-tell ships?"

He said, "I'll tell you what. It's 'don't-ask, don't-tell' if you get the hell off my ship. You're not about to handle my ship!"

"Now, Captain, don't get excited," I said.

"Don't tell me not to get excited. I'm a commander in the United States Navy."

I said, "Okay." With that, I removed the wig, wiped off the lipstick, smiled and said, "Well, let's get underway."

The captain started to laugh. "You SOB," he said. "I have never had anybody pull anything like this on me."

I said, "Well, I just wanted to lighten things up."

I had the ship out at sea in 30 minutes.

The next time the tanker went through, the Navy captain made a point of requesting that I be his pilot.

24. Alcohol counseling

For a long time, drinking was a part of the maritime culture. The industry was notorious for the availability of alcohol for those working on ships. Pilots were part of that culture. It was not uncommon for the captain of a vessel to break open a bottle of whiskey and share a drink with a pilot right before they got underway. It was so prevalent that some pilots on the Panama Canal assumed drinking on the job was okay until maritime regulations in the 1970s strictly prohibited it. In many places, though, the rules were largely overlooked.

When I worked on the canal in the 1980s, we had one pilot who was caught drinking on the job. His supervisors removed him from the ship, and then covered up the incident. Nobody ever disciplined the pilots who drank unless they were involved in a serious accident.

After work, Panama Canal pilots used to hang out at a club someone had built in the nearby mountains. Many went there after working 14 hours straight. They'd grab a paper cup full of whiskey to medicate themselves so they could sleep.

Often, I'd say to pilots after a shift, "Guys, I got to go home." They'd say, "Well, we're going up to the club." And then they'd spend two or three days there. It wasn't just the booze that lured them. The club had become something of a den of iniquity where pilots brought in ladies of the night.

On many occasions when a pilot was intoxicated at the club, someone called a taxi to get him home. The pilot sometimes would wake up the next morning to find he didn't have as much money in his wallet as he thought he should. This happened enough times that the pilots began to suspect a certain Panamanian taxi driver was the culprit.

The pilots formulated a theory that the cabbie would pickpocket the pilot's wallet when he got into the back of the cab. Then the cabbie would help himself to a few extra bucks before he helpfully walked the pilot to his front door and handed him his wallet, telling him he found it on the floor of the cab.

Nobody could prove there was any thievery going on. But some of the older pilots decided to take the matter into their own hands in the belief it would send a message to all Panamanian taxi drivers. When the cabbie showed up one night at the club, two of the pilots pretended to kidnap a third pilot. They threw him in the back of the taxi. Then they told the cabbie the man had stolen money from them and they were going to get revenge.

"Take us to the cane fields. We're going to kill this SOB," one told the cabbie. "Don't you say anything either or we'll shoot you, too."

The cabbie's eyes got big, and he began protesting. The pilots continued to demand he drive them to the cane fields. Afraid for his own safety, the cabbie did just that.

While he sat in the cab, the two pilots dragged their "victim" out of sight of the taxi. One of the pilots fired off a starter pistol a couple of times in their mock execution. A few minutes later, the first two pilots got back into the taxi and ordered the cabbie, now a nervous wreck, to drive them back to the club. Someone picked up the third pilot from the cane fields, and all the pilots later congratulated themselves on a well-played prank. They hoped this would solve the problem of alleged thievery.

Meanwhile, the cabbie flagged down a couple of Panama Canal policemen. He told them that two pilots inside that club shot and killed a guy out in the cane fields. "I don't want anything to do with it," he reportedly told the police.

The police in the canal area began an investigation and gathered a group of people to search the cane field. When they didn't find anything, they accused the taxi driver of lying. The pilots insisted they had no idea what the cabbie was talking about.

The club used the incident to ban that cabbie from picking up more fares there. Word of the fake shooting eventually leaked to canal authorities. But they hushed it up to avoid a scandal. The pilots were never disciplined for their little stunt.

***

Drinking on ships by officers and crew pretty much disappeared overnight following the Exxon Valdez accident in Alaska in 1990. The oil tanker ran aground off Alaska and spilled all that oil that devastated the coastline. The captain was cleared of allegations he had been drinking that night. However, that accident was a turning point for compliance with rules regarding drinking in the maritime industry. After that governments and shipping companies decided that enough was enough. They closed all the bars on ships for crew members. They eliminated alcohol on American and British cargo ships. The new policies filtered into piloting guidelines.

Still, pilots being pilots and alcoholics being alcoholics, drinking continued. I didn't drink. But from my own family experience and from my training in the military, I knew alcoholism was a tough thing to break. Once it gets ahold of you, it never lets go. It's just as bad as cocaine or any of the drugs out there. It's a living thing. Once it's alive and established, some people never get rid of it.

After he became Panama Canal's chief pilot, Don Garrido called me one day. He found out that I had been certified as an alcohol counselor and had worked with guys in the military with drinking problems. He asked if there was anything I could do to help Panama Canal pilots, executives and other senior employees who had alcohol problems.

Sure, I said. "If you have an employee in the marine division that has a problem, call me. I'll see what I can do."

I discovered over the years that a lot of the people who had alcohol issues were well-educated individuals with families. They were good people. But educated people often are the last to admit they have any kind of problem. They frequently don't seek help until in serious trouble.

Panama Canal Deputy Administrator Raymond P. Lavery presents me with the Panama Canal Commission's Silver Medal for Public Service during a ceremony in 1993 at the commission headquarters.

When I provided counseling to Panama Canal employees, I did so in private. In 1993, word of my effort became public only after Captain Garrido recommended me for the Panama Canal Commission Silver Medal for Public Service, which I was presented at a ceremony. The award was described as honoring "dedicated service in working with members of the community who have become victims of alcohol and drug use."

Although grateful for the honor, I felt it was Captain Garrido who deserved it for recognizing the drinking problem and taking steps to combat it.

25. Darlene

I attended a seminar in Ohio in 1987 as I was formulating a plan to start another nautical training and consulting company. Visiting Cincinnati also gave me a chance to spend time with my sister, Barbara, and her two children. At the seminar, I met a woman about my age, Darlene Somerlot. She was there representing the Ohio Joint Vocational School, where she was a work and family coordinator. Darlene and I hit it off right away, and before long I was commuting to Ohio on my four weeks off to visit my sister and to spend time with Darlene. On July 28, 1989, Darlene and I got married, and I made my U.S. residence with her in Bellefontaine, Ohio, while commuting to Panama. I never did set up that nautical school.

Not long after we got married, Darlene accompanied me for a visit to Panama. We got off the plane about 9 o'clock at night and were met by Morgan, a Panamanian friend who worked for the commission as a launch supervisor. Morgan picked us up at the airport in the Mitsubishi Lancer I owned. After putting our luggage in the car, I got behind the wheel because Morgan didn't like to drive at night. Morgan slipped into the front seat with me. Darlene got in the back.

We had no sooner left the airport when, at a stoplight, both back doors opened, and two Panamanian policemen jumped in, one on each side of Darlene. I was looking in the rearview mirror when this happened, and I could see Darlene's eyes were as big as quarters.

One of the cops said, "Take us downtown." He gave us the name of a restaurant in Panama City.

I said, *"Seguro que no hay problema!"* Which is essentially Spanish for I'll do whatever you tell me to do. Darlene didn't really know what I said. She just kept quiet, but I could see she was just beside herself. She couldn't believe a couple of Guardia had commandeered our car.

We got to the next intersection and, believe it or not, two more police officers flagged us down. They approached the vehicle, ready to open the back doors and get in. But they saw the two policemen already in there, so they waved us off.

By the time we got to the restaurant, Darlene was terrified, but she still hadn't said a word. I turned around and thanked the officers for escorting us, and I gave them $5 each for dinner. They got out, and that was the end of it. But at that point, Darlene was ready to return to the airport and go back to Ohio.

***

Such incidents had become all too common in Panama by the late-1980s. General Noriega's Guardia had started backing away from protecting citizens in favor of shaking down locals and running illegal drugs. The lawlessness in Panama was about as blatant as you could get. One time when Darlene and I were at the Panama airport, a guy got off a plane from Colombia carrying four bags stuffed with cash. I'm guessing it was drug money. It took him an hour to deposit the cash in a bank in the airport. As we waited, Darlene joked, "Can't we hit him over the head?"

Corruption was everywhere in Panama, not just among Noriega's police forces. It had seeped into every aspect of government life. When you wanted to register your car, you had to go to a fellow by the name of Mingo. He went to a government office and did the job for you. Car registration was $14, but you had to give Mingo $34 and he pocketed the difference. If you tried to avoid Mingo, there were people in Panama who could make your car disappear. Of course, some hard-nosed Americans new to Panama would tell me, "I'm not paying anybody anything to register my car for me." I would say, "You're no longer in the U.S. You're not in Kansas anymore. This is Panama. It's a foreign country, and they run the show."

There wasn't much the Panama Canal Commission could do about the corruption. After the United States signed the treaties, the Panamanians had taken over almost all security the former Canal Zone.

Almost every morning, Darlene looked out the window of our apartment, and there would be a Panamanian policeman sitting on the patio. I had a maid at the time who gave him coffee and an egg sandwich. Darlene was uneasy knowing a policeman was outside waiting for his breakfast. I said, "What are you complaining about? It just means we got a little more police protection. And all it costs us is an egg and a cup of coffee. He's not going to do anything crazy. He knows who we are and what we do."

One time, Darlene took some papers over to the U.S. Army base and she drove through downtown to get there. After I returned from work about 5 o'clock in the afternoon, our car was in the driveway with its right side torn up. Darlene explained she was struck at an intersection by a driver who ran a stop sign in a stolen car. Fortunately, she wasn't hurt.

We ended up in court over who would pay for the damages. Our lawyer argued the man who stole the car should pay. The woman who owned the stolen car wanted us to pay because we had money and the "bigger car." For a minute, I thought the judge was going to rule in her favor. But he said, "No, both of you pay for your own car." My lawyer was ready to object, but I quietly told him, "The judge has ruled. Do not say anything. If you open your mouth, we're going to have to take care of both cars."

***

Despite the hassles, Darlene and I liked to eat in downtown Panama because the food there was so good. But before we headed out, I'd call the restaurant and ask, "Do you have tablecloths?" If I was told it had three or four per table, we went there to dinner. Tablecloths were important because criminals used to come into the restaurants with shotguns and rob the patrons. After a while, the women stopped wearing their valuable jewelry, and the guys would stop carrying cash in favor of only a credit card. With nothing else valuable to steal, the crooks made patrons strip and then stole all their clothing. That's why I made the call to the restaurant to ensure it had enough tablecloths for us to wrap around ourselves if robbers showed up.

As crime and other tensions worsened, the Panama Canal pilots union demanded that the United States do more to protect us from harassment by government soldiers. In 1988, the U.S. Senate passed a resolution urging President Reagan to use economic sanctions to pressure Noriega into resigning. It didn't work. Noriega also rejected an offer to go into exile in Spain in exchange for the U.S. not pursuing drug-trafficking charges.

By 1989, as the U.S. tightened economic sanctions on Panama, there were cash and food shortages and many government functions shut down. Somehow, the canal remained operational.

***

During one visit to Panama, Darlene said, "Ken, I want to go on a transit."

I said, "Okay, honey. I'm getting up at 3 in the morning. You can get up with me, and we'll take the pilot's launch to a ship waiting in the bay."

We got into a launch on our way to this cargo ship just as the sun was rising.

"How am I going to get aboard?" she asked.

I said, "You climb the pilot's ladder."

When we got to the ship, she stared at the filthy 30-foot rope ladder. She looked at me as if to say: Why didn't you tell me about the ladder?

But, God love her, she went right up that ladder. If she fell, so would I, because I was right behind her. We finally made it to the bridge. As we had a cup of coffee, she was still giving me the evil eye.

Then I received a radio call from marine traffic control.

"Captain Puckett? That ship has been canceled. You're going to have to get off the ship and board another one."

Down the same ladder we went, stepped into the launch, then climbed one on the other ship. Darlene was right there with me. But after that, she never made another transit unless it was on a cruise ship.

Even when she didn't join me for a transit, Darlene would often come up to the locks early in the morning and sit on the hood of a car with a cup of coffee to watch my ship come through. She waved, and I waved back.

One morning when I was sure she would be sitting there, a character that I am, I told this Greek captain that I was a little worried.

"Geez, I don't know what I'm going to do, Captain."

He said, "Why is that? What are you worried about?"

I said, "I'm being stalked. I have this blonde woman who follows me around."

We arrived at the locks and, sure enough, there was Darlene on the hood of the car waving at me. I said to the captain, "See, I told you."

He apparently liked what he saw, because he tooted the ship's whistle – *Whoo! Whoo! Whoo!* And he said, "Do you think I could meet her?" He still didn't know she was my wife, and I didn't tell him.

I said, "Sure, but you'll have to take her out to dinner, and I better go along just to be safe."

He came through the canal again, but I never was able to work out a free dinner with the captain and Darlene.

26. The invasion

BY late 1989, Panama was in a full-blown crisis. Federal grand juries in Florida had indicted Noriega for drug smuggling and money laundering. The U.S. stopped turning over to Panama the income taxes the canal collected from Panamanians working as pilots for the canal. Noriega responded by summoning the pilots and threatening to seize their houses and bank accounts if they didn't pay the money themselves.

The shakedowns by police worsened. One time I was heading to the airport with Morgan when we were stopped by police, who as usual demanded money. Morgan tried to argue, but I told him to just hand over the cash. It wasn't worth risking arrest, or worse, for a few dollars. I always made sure I never carried more than $20 because that seemed to be enough to appease the crooked cops. Noriega's Panamanian Defense Forces (PDF) even harassed U.S. troops. Some members of the Air National Guard visiting from the United States went for a walk, wound up against a wall and had their wallets taken.

Both the U.S. and Panama imposed curfews until somebody remembered that the canal operated 24/7 and that canal personnel needed to get to work at all hours. The canal commission then told us that we weren't subject to the curfew. All we had to do was show our identification if we were stopped. Of course, that just gave the PDF more chances to extort money from us.

The U.S. Marines began to carry out nightly maneuvers in Panama in a show of force. It was unnerving to hear small-arms fire and mortars every night. There were 1,500 Americans and 2,000 Panamanians working in the former Canal Zone, all unarmed, caught between two potentially combative groups. I was worried that a serviceman with an itchy trigger finger might set off a gun battle at any minute. It didn't matter if he was an American or a Panamanian.

I left for Bellefontaine on December 3, 1989, for my four-week rotation back to the States. Two weeks later, a U.S. Marine was shot to death at a PDF roadblock. With that, President George H.W. Bush had enough. He ordered a U.S. invasion, which began December 20 as "Operation Just Cause."

About 9,000 U.S. troops arrived to assist 12,000 already in Panama to overthrow Noriega and restore order. I was still home in Ohio when the invasion of Panama occurred. In an interview with *Columbus (Ohio) Dispatch* staff reporter Jim Massie, I blurted out what he referred to as a "colorful adjective" to describe the horrendous conditions in recent months for those living and working in Panama amid all the threats and counter-threats.

"It was a constant escalation," I told him. "It was a tit-for-tat, back-and-forth kind of thing. You knock this chip off my shoulder, I'll knock that one off yours."

The morning of the invasion, the U.S. military boarded pilot boats and stopped the canal from operating for a day or so. It was the only time in Panama Canal's history that it was closed for more than 24 hours.

Many of the pilots were upset because a small group of canal administrators, including the marine director – an ex-Navy captain – and some port captains knew of the invasion, but they never warned the employees. They sent pilots out to work that morning in launches, knowing they could be in harm's way.

At 5 a.m., a Navy Swift Boat pulled alongside a pilot boat. Armed U.S. Navy personnel boarded the pilot boat and held the American pilots and crew at gunpoint as if they were criminals.

Based on the information I had while in Ohio, I thought the United States military action had been pretty "surgical" to avoid civilian casualties. Later, after talking to pilots when I returned to Panama, my opinion changed. The Pentagon publicly claimed that 516 Panamanians were killed. When I talked to an American lawyer representing Panamanians, he estimated that over 3,000 people lost their lives. He said that only 173 of those were military combatants from both sides. Among the civilian casualties were two American schoolteachers who worked for the Department of Defense Schools in Panama. Friendly fire killed another American who ran a roadblock. After the invasions, there were mass burials of Panamanians.

Flames engulf a building after clashes between Panamanian Defense Forces and the United States military during "Operation Just Cause" in late December 1989. (Photo from the U.S. National Archives.)

Fighting and fires destroyed huge swaths of Panama City. Just two blocks from my house in the former Canal Zone, a police station was completely gutted. Some city blocks had so much destruction that the American military decided to level them with bulldozers.

Noriega briefly eluded U.S. forces but was finally captured January 3, 1990. He was brought back to the U.S., convicted, and spent the rest of his life behind bars. I know plenty of people in Panama were happy Noriega was driven out of power. But the way the military invasion was carried out left a sour taste for many.

***

Right after the invasion, Panama democratically elected a new leader. It dissolved the old Panamanian police force and swore in new officers.

Even so, for a while, living in Panama seemed almost as perilous as before the invasion. *The Arizona Daily Star* reported in September 1990 that Panama City police revealed that the rate of crime, especially armed robberies, had soared. One American couple told the newspaper that their home had been burglarized several times since December 1989. Eventually, though, things simmered down and life in Panama stabilized.

In 1993, Darlene came to live with me in Panama. While there, she attended the University of Oklahoma's Advanced Studies Program offered on the U.S. military bases in Panama. In 1995, she earned a master's degree in educational psychology from the university. She also worked for the university as a graduate school enrollment specialist.

Meanwhile, tired of the Ohio winters, we moved our home in the States to Florida.

I predicted to the *Dispatch* reporter in December 1989 that the canal's future wasn't in jeopardy, regardless of whether there were any remaining troops loyal to Noriega or whether a leader friendly to the United States took over. With the turnover of the canal still scheduled for the end of 1999, few in Panama wanted to do anything to jeopardize that.

"I would term the canal a demilitarized zone," I said. "I don't think anybody will mess with it. There would be international implications, and it would be a treaty violation. That would be detrimental to Panama."

But lingering instability kept many of us worried that Panama would not be ready to assume control of the canal at the end of the decade.

27. Bananas

I was off-duty for four weeks in Panama around the early 1990s when I got a call from an agent for a shipping company. He explained he needed help disposing of several thousand tons of ripened bananas. The bananas had been loaded in Ecuador aboard a refrigerated cargo ship destined for the East Coast of the United States and for Europe.

Bananas are always picked green, then put in a cargo hold maintained close to freezing so that the fruit didn't ripen too early. In the case of this cargo ship, the refrigeration system failed, and the bananas started to ripen prematurely. The ship's insurance company had condemned the whole lot.

The agent explained, "By the time we get through the canal, the bananas will be ruined. We won't be able to sell them."

The company put the word out in Panama that if anyone wanted free bananas, come to the pier and get them. Even my maid picked up 100 pounds of bananas. I think we made banana bread for a week.

The agent hired a couple of Panamanian cargo gangs, took the ship with the remaining bananas 30 miles out to the ocean and jettisoned them over the side. It took them five days to dump those bananas.

About two or three days later, I boarded an American tanker coming from the West Coast. I was assigned as the control pilot on the Pacific side; a second pilot handled the last half of the transit.

We boarded about 3 or 4 in the morning. I greeted the captain, a longtime friend, and we started talking.

He said, "God, Ken, I think I'm going crazy. I just came through the Bay of Panama and went through a sea of bananas."

"Really?"

Apparently, the bananas didn't decompose very quickly in saltwater, and just continued to float on the surface for a while.

I kept a straight face. "Boy, you're in big trouble," I said. "That's how we grow bananas in Panama, didn't you know that?"

"I didn't know that," the captain said.

"Yeah, we have aquafarming. We grow bananas in the sea. If you went through that sea of bananas, you went through our aquafarm and you're in a lot of trouble. You could get fined if they find out about this."

The captain had a look of panic by then.

"Well, what the heck am I going to do?" he asked.

I told the American captain that if he gave me a case of booze from his slop chest, I could give it to Panamanian authorities in exchange for not pursuing a fine.

"You will do that?" the captain asked.

"Sure," I said, "I can handle that."

When I got off the ship on the other end of the canal, he lowered some bottles of whiskey to me. The other pilot looked at me and said, "What the heck is this?"

I said, "You don't need to know. Don't worry about it. I did a heck of a job on the other side."

Since I didn't drink, I donated the bottles to the union hall and didn't think anything more about it.

About a week later, the same American tanker came from Galveston going the other way. Different pilots were assigned to the ship this time.

The captain told one of them, "I want to see Puckett. You tell that SOB I want to talk to him."

Later, one of the pilots said to me, "Boy, are you in trouble. The captain on that tanker figured out what you pulled on him with the bananas."

"What did he say?"

"He said he was about a half-hour out at sea when he realized they don't grow bananas in the ocean."

I made a point to avoid being assigned to that tanker the next time it came though.

***

In the early 1990s, I was assigned part time to the port captains' office. There were six to eight port captains working 24 hours a day to coordinate the operations on both sides of the canal. They made sure that the right pilot was on the right ship and that management assigned pilots according to their qualifications and seniority.

In 1994, I became the first person on the Panama Canal appointed to be a supervisory pilot, a quasi-management position. The job was created in part to ease growing turmoil among those American pilots who continued to resist turnover of the canal. The transition included appointing a Panamanian, Fernando Manfredo, to succeed General McAuliffe as administrator of the Panama Canal Commission.

In this photo scanned from a June 1990 issue of Panama Canal newsletter The Spillway, I present Captain Earle H. Holder with an autographed photo of Detroit Tigers manager Sparky Anderson during a party commemorating the end of Captain Holder's 50-year career with the Panama Canal.

The marine director decided that, because I was a senior pilot with experience training others and working as a union official, I might bridge the gap between management and pilots. The supervisory pilot's job was intended to be that of a peacekeeper, if you will – although in that position my responsibilities were mostly those of a port captain.

It was a nightmare.

We had a few pilots who were prima donnas. They thought they were better than they really were. One came to work, called me on the radio and said, "The ship's captain is smoking on the bridge. I'm not taking this ship through the canal." Another said, "There's a toilet not working." Just nickel-dime stuff.

There were always a few pilots who thought they were more important than the operation. They did not understand ships coming through the canal were paying our salaries indirectly through the tolls, and we had a responsibility to work together to get the ship through in a timely manner

Fortunately, only about ten pilots caused much trouble. The rest professionally completed their assignments and didn't get upset about petty stuff.

28. Sarah Terry

PILOTING was, and still is, a tough field for women to break into. It wasn't until the 1970s when I was attending New York Maritime College that it enrolled its first female cadets. Still, we were a year ahead of the U.S. Naval Academy, which didn't accept women applicants until 1976. Of the seven original Maritime College female cadets, I think two ended up in piloting careers. The U.S. lagged much of the world on this. Europeans have always allowed women crew members aboard ships and integrated them into the maritime officer corps.

The first woman to become a pilot on the Panama Canal was Sarah Terry, a Massachusetts native who worked her way up through the system when the U.S. ran the canal, breaking down barriers all the way.

She got her foot in the door as the canal's first female machinist's apprentice in the 1970s. A 2001 profile in *Cruising World* magazine details how she subsequently joined the tugboat mate apprentice program over objections of some who thought life on the tugs – including their grungy bathrooms – was too rough for a woman. She insisted on applying for the job, and she soon impressed everyone with her attitude and competence.

"The moment the men realized that I wasn't worried about breaking a nail and that I would be out on deck come rain or shine, slinging three-inch hawsers with the best of them, they became my greatest supporters," she told *Cruising World.*

Panama Canal pilot Sarah Terry, walkie-talkie in hand, is seen in this June 1988 photo scanned from canal newsletter The Spillway.

In 1983, she passed all the standard exams to become the first woman licensed tugboat captain on the canal. Captain Terry didn't stop there. In 1986, she successfully applied for the Panama Canal pilot apprentice training program and eventually became a Step Eight pilot, a position shared by only 130 people at the time.

She had no trouble mixing it up with the guys. Captain Charlie McDaniels, another pilot, told me about the time he went aboard a Japanese ship with Captain Terry and a young Panamanian pilot apprentice.

They were standing there having coffee when Charlie said to the ship's captain, "I'm going to let my wife take the ship through the canal."

The captain said, "Who?"

"My wife."

"Oh, no, your wife cannot take the ship."

"It's okay. She's my wife. She travels with me all the time."

Captain Terry got on the radio and said, "This is North 7. I'm ready to get underway."

The Japanese captain said, "No, we don't want her."

So, Captain Terry said, "OK, then I'll let my son do it." And she handed the radio to the young Panamanian apprentice.

It was only then that Charlie revealed to the ship's captain that Sarah indeed was a qualified ship pilot. With that, they successfully completed the transit.

Sarah Terry later became a port captain and continued to work on the canal until early retirement on February 22, 2001.

29. The yacht accident

TAKING a yacht through the Panama Canal could be very tricky. These ships are thin-hulled with exteriors generally made of fiberglass. A pilot aboard a yacht needed to take his time and understand the proper transit procedures. It was unfortunate that the canal almost always assigned a junior pilot for the delicate task of taking these vessels through the locks.

One day while I was training as a port captain, a yacht was transiting the locks in the same chamber as a big ship. We did this often for the sake of efficiency, rather than move a yacht through by itself. The big ship would enter the locks first, followed by a tug placed along the wall. Once the tug was secured, the yacht would be tied to it to prevent the yacht's hull from being damaged.

In this case, someone mistakenly placed the yacht between a wall and the heavy tugboat. Predictably, when the water entered the chamber, the tug lurched and crushed the yacht against the concrete wall. The bottom fell out of the yacht, and its motor went right to the bottom.

The yacht owner, three passengers and four Panamanians line handlers who were aboard all leaped onto the tugboat, escaping seconds before the yacht disappeared under the water. No one was hurt.

When we heard about the accident, we arranged for a boat to pick up the owner and his three passengers. The port captain immediately tried to calm the owner.

"You lost your yacht," he told him. "Obviously, this is our fault. We take responsibility for this."

The canal paid for the owner and passengers to stay at a hotel. Meanwhile, we obtained the yacht's certification number to access U.S. Coast Guard records on the vessel's specifications and its equipment. We also determined the name of the insurance company.

We also interviewed the owner and asked him to complete an accident claim form.

"You will be reimbursed for the loss of the yacht. And you need to list anything you left on board in order for us to compute the final compensation for your loss," a port captain told him.

The owner sat down and listed a couple of radars and radios and some personal effects, including two fur coats owned by his wife. He then added that the ship had gold bullion worth $20,000 stored under the engine.

When he returned the claim form, the port captain looked at it and said, "You realize when you sign this, it's notarized, and you are filing a federal claim against the U.S. government. You're certifying that the statement in these papers is correct."

"Yeah, yeah. I know. I know," the yacht owner said.

We weren't sure if he got the point. "You understand that if it's incorrect," the port captain said, "if you're lying and making a false claim, you could lose everything."

"That's okay," he said.

The port captain pressed on. "One other thing you need to know. When we pulled that yacht out of the locks right after the accident, we didn't find two fur coats or bullion underneath that engine. You sure you don't want to change your claim?"

At that point, the owner asked to have the form back. He crossed off the fur coats and the gold bullion.

With that, we authorized a check for $115,000 for his losses. Right there, right then.

30. The Trump Princess

I was informed in a phone call in the early 1990s that I was assigned to pilot a yacht. I was surprised, of course, because senior pilots rarely handled small vessels.

"Why are you giving me a yacht?"

"It's a big yacht," I was told. "It's the Trump Princess."

The Trump Princess was a luxury "superyacht" owned by Donald Trump when he was best known as a wealthy real estate developer in New York City. News reports say Trump spent close to $30 million in 1988 to purchase the 282-foot yacht from Saudi billionaire Adam Khashoggi. Trump got a pretty good deal. Reportedly, when the yacht was launched in 1980, it had cost about $100 million.

The yacht had five decks and was truly spectacular – a gleaming white boat with luxury inside and out. Cabin walls were covered in chamois leather and bird's eye maple. Bathrooms were done in onyx hand-carved by Italian craftsmen. Trump once said he bought the yacht because it was a "great piece of art at a ridiculously low price."

Following a real-estate recession in 1990, Trump decided to sell the boat to Saudi Prince al-Waleed bin Talal for an estimated $20 million. The yacht's crew of 12 was now running the Trump Princess through the Panama Canal on its way to its new owner.

We started off early in the morning in Cristobal. It didn't take long to figure out what the ship could do and what it couldn't. It had a lot of power, but it was made of very lightweight materials. Everyone was concerned about putting a hole in the hull as it went through the locks. We couldn't use the regular cables on the locomotives to guide the ship because they might yank the whole ship apart; it would pull the fittings right off. So, we had to use special nylon lines attached to the locomotives to keep the yacht away from the wall.

We got through the Gatun Locks with no problem, and by 10 o'clock we were making the slow transit across the lake. The captain had his wife aboard for the trip, and everyone was very friendly and professional. The food was fabulous, too. I was told I could have anything I wanted for lunch. I jokingly said, "I'd like some wiener schnitzel," and the captain said, "No problem. My wife will fix some for you," and she did.

As we crossed the canal, I had time to chat with the captain, and he shared that he had been working for Trump on the Princess for a couple of years. The crew had to be ready for Trump 24 hours a day, seven days a week. The boat was moored in New York harbor, right off LaGuardia Airport.

The captain said he periodically would get a phone call from Trump saying, "I'm coming down today. I want to get underway."

About a year before the Princess was sold, Trump called for his yacht. He was told the captain was not available. He and his wife had taken their son to a hospital on Long Island after the boy became critically ill. When Trump found out, he contacted the captain at the hospital and said, "Look, you bring your boy to the airport. We're going to put him on my jet and fly him to the Cleveland Clinic for children. That's one of the best children's hospitals in the United States. And we're going to pay for it 100 percent. I can't have one of my employees' children having a problem we don't take care of."

Trump did what he promised, and the boy received the critical care paid for by Trump.

The captain told me, "Mr. Trump can tell me to go to China and back for nothing and I would do it for nothing because of the kind of person he is."

When I finished the transit, the captain handed me a baseball cap that had "Trump Princess" on the brim. He also gave me a box of

Trump matchbooks and a stash of wine with the Trump name on the bottles.

Years later, when I lectured on cruise ships, I would tell this story about Trump and how he helped the captain's sick boy. Some of the passengers got on my case about it, even though this was well before Trump was elected president. I said, "Hey, it's a story. I got it from the captain, and he said Trump was a fantastic employer. I mean, what can I say? I'm just sharing the situation with you."

After Trump became president, I had one of the cruise lines inform me not to tell this story anymore. Trump had just become too controversial, and cruise ships don't like anything political that might upset passengers.

31. Captain Puckett goes to Washington

By the middle of the 1990s, I began to consider retirement from piloting. I was closing in on 55 years old. By the time a pilot reaches that age, he has no business climbing those slippery pilot ladders. I was beginning to lose strength in my arms and legs. I also felt the strain of night work, long hours and some of the internal strife among the American pilots over union issues. I just didn't want to deal with it anymore.

In 1996, I asked to come off the supervisory pilot's job. I went back to working as a full-time senior pilot for my last couple of months on the job.

That July, I piloted my last ship through the canal after more than 1,400 transits. This time it was the Radisson Diamond, a 455-foot passenger cruise ship with an odd design resembling a huge catamaran. Darlene accompanied me for this final transit. The next day, the union gave me a Panama Canal pilot's clock as a traditional retirement gift. We packed up and came home to Florida.

In a final bit of housekeeping, I sent a letter of appreciation to the drivers who transported the pilots across the isthmus to and from their assignments. "Like pilots, their hours are not always routine, and they also have problems getting enough sleep before work," I wrote. "In many respects, I believe their jobs, at times, were more difficult than mine had been."

For a while after I left piloting, I tried not to think too much about the Panama Canal. One thing I learned from the military was: When you leave a job, you move on. You don't linger on what happened yesterday. You move to the next challenge.

We returned to Florida. We traveled. We relaxed in our new retirement home. I prepared to do more teaching of maritime licensing.

But as the pending turnover of the canal approached in 1999, I began to have growing worries about the plan to leave such a vital waterway in the hands of a third-world country.

One of my fears was that the Panamanian government – although it would be a legally separate entity from the pending Panama Canal Authority – might try to siphon off the canal revenues destined for operational costs and upkeep. Without funds for proper upkeep, the canal might go down the tubes.

A second fear was that Panama might sell the canal to another nation, such as Japan or China. Such a move would guarantee Panama billions of dollars off the top without having to operate the canal. It was chilling to contemplate a communist nation such as China controlling access to the Panama Canal.

A third worry was that China or Iran might try to build an alternative canal in Nicaragua, which would be a disaster not only economically for the Panama Canal but could also trigger ecological problems for Central America.

I was not alone in my concerns.

Yes, there were some in the U.S. military who thought: Hand over the canal. We don't need it. We have no use for it. It costs us. We can't get through there anyway with most of our newer Navy ships.

On the other side, there was a group of naval officers led by retired Admiral Thomas Moore, former chairman of the Joint Chiefs of Staff. They wanted the United States to essentially tear up the treaties and keep the canal. Moore argued that the canal remained a tactical part of the U.S. defense system, that we needed an Army and Navy presence in Panama keeping an eye on who was using the canal and for what purposes. He also was deeply concerned the Chinese would worm their way into operational control of the canal at the expense of other nations. Even if the Panamanians retained formal ownership of the canal, Moore and other naval officers argued, America should have indirect control just by our presence.

In 1999, I began working with retired Navy Captain Jack Griffin, who was also a former Panama Canal pilot. I helped Jack write position papers on the turnover of the Panama Canal. He planned that December to personally present one paper to the U.S. House of Representatives Subcommittee on Domestic and International Monetary Policy, which was examining the financial, commercial and security implications of handing over the canal to Panama.

On December 5, Jack became ill and asked that I finish the paper and then go to Washington three days later. All I would have to do was hand over the written testimony to the subcommittee. I agreed.

The plan was for Admiral Moore and Army Lt. Gen. Gordon Sumner to read their own statements and testify in person to the committee. However, instead of me being merely an observer, I was kind of sandbagged. One congressman – I can't think of his name now – said, "Come with me." We walked down the hall, he opened a door, and there we were in the hearing room. He said, "Read the paper you and Captain Griffin prepared into the Congressional Record." And that's what I did, and then stuck around to answer questions.

Moore told the hearing that the United States was permitting "the communist Chinese a foothold" by not stopping a Hong Kong company from operating two canal ports. He argued that China could use those facilities to launch missiles at the U.S.

General Sumner raised fears that Chinese and Latin American terrorists would attempt to disrupt traffic through the canal. He complained that it had been foolish for the United States to agree to give up its military bases on Panama. "I view this as part of the disarming of America, not just militarily, but economically," he said.

The points made by Captain Griffin and me weren't quite so incendiary. Our statement focused more on explaining the physical condition and operation of the canal.

In my testimony, I also made it clear I was neither disparaging the Panama Canal Commission nor the Panamanian workers taking over the operation.

"As a senior canal pilot," I said, "I am frequently asked if I think Panama can operate the Panama Canal once they assume control on 31 December 1999. I have always answered in the affirmative. There are hundreds of men and women in Panama well-qualified to manage and operate the canal if given that opportunity."

However, after the hearing, I heard from several Panamanians who were upset about my appearance, assuming I testified against them.

I said, "No I didn't. I didn't testify against you. Read what I said. Read it."

Shortly after 10 a.m., in Room 2128 of the Rayburn House Office Building, with Admiral Moore on one side and a four-star Army general on the other, I read the prepared statement and then answered questions from Representative Spencer Bachus of Alabama, chairman of the subcommittee.

"It is not often that a seaman on watch is called to the pilothouse to offer his opinion on the course of the ship, and I thank you for that," I told the chairman.

In my statement and during my comments in the subsequent question-and-answer session, I made several key points:

· The Panama Canal in 1999 was showing its age, despite better lighting, new locomotives and other improvements over the years. The canal was allowing the larger Panamax ships to squeeze through the canal, adding to deterioration of the locks. "Each time a Panamax vessel is forced into a lock chamber," I told the committee, "the whole structure begins to vibrate. It is these vibrations that concern me. Cracks can be observed in the concrete lock walls, and the steel miter gates leak. A breach of the lock walls and internal culverts or a miter gate failure could close the Panama Canal for an indefinite period of time."

· I expressed concern that the demands of a growing population in Panama, along with the nation's commercial expansion, could prompt its leaders to try to siphon off electricity from the canal's generating plant, jeopardizing canal operations.

· I told the committee that changes planned by Panama to allow preferred scheduling of canal transits might "foster a bidding war among these shipping agents, shipping companies, vessel owners, and even countries for that matter," plus put in jeopardy the strategic requirements of the U.S. military.

· One of my other major concerns was that the newly formed Panama Canal Authority was planning to require vessel owners to assume liability for damages caused by canal pilots and canal employees. I feared that this change would prompt some ship captains to literally battle the pilots to maintain navigational control during transits. "Imagine for a moment the chaos in the cockpit of a 747 jumbo jet with two pilots fighting for control of an aircraft during a landing. I have experienced this (kind of battle) six times in my life on the canal, and I had full navigational control," I said.

· Finally, I urged that the Panama Canal be viewed as a "world utility" and that the United States should take the lead to do whatever was required to keep it open for all nations.

***

Looking back now, nearly two decades later, I don't think our testimony that day led to any changes related to the handover of the canal. By then, it was probably too late.

But some of the fears I expressed then have come to pass. Records show, true to form, there was some corruption at the highest level of the Panamanian government right after the canal was turned over. However, the honest, practical government politicians in Panama realized the dangers and stepped in. They enacted additional laws that kept the Panama Canal Authority independent and autonomous. Because of that, to this day, the Panama Canal operates totally independent of other agencies of the Panamanian government. The authority is only required to provide a percentage of its profits, if any, to the Panamanian government. The only real influence the Panamanian government has over the canal is in the selection of the director of the authority.

While tolls have skyrocketed, the canal remains open and independent and available to all countries of the world. So, in a practical sense, Panama has treated the canal as world utility as I recommended in my testimony.

An aerial view of the expanded Panama Canal and its new Agua Clara Locks on the Atlantic Ocean side of Panama on January 12, 2017. (Photo from the U.S. Department of Transportation.)

Panamanians have worked hard since 2000 to modernize the canal, adding to its capacity as part of a $5.3 billion project completed in fall of 2016. The work included construction of additional sets of lock chambers larger than the old ones – each 1,400 feet long, 180 feet wide and 60 feet deep. The canal came up with the name Neopanamax to classify ships too large for the old locks but capable of transiting through the new ones.

Like all large government construction projects, there were cost overruns, mishandling of contract bids and some poor decisions about materials, including substandard concrete. However, the expanded locks were key to bringing the canal into the 21st century. The new locks' innovative basin system using recycled water from the lake helps to ease concerns about conserving Panama's delicate watershed.

A lot of Americans don't realize the United States not only turned over the canal to the Panamanians. We also turned over the former Canal Zone, that 55-mile-long strip of land that bisected Panama. Under the original Panama Canal Treaty and U.S. government law, commercial business operations were prohibited while the U.S. military controlled that Zone.

In the years since Panama took over, this land has become an area with maritime, petroleum and commercial operations. Balboa and Cristobal have been converted into major Central American commercial port operations with thousands of tons of cargo flowing through Panama. The northern shores of Panama on the Caribbean will soon be home to one of the largest petroleum and chemical refinery operations in the hemisphere. This is all great for the economy and independence of Panama. None of this would have happened if the U.S. had not turned over the Panama Canal and the adjoining land.

On the downside, I think there are reasons to remain concerned that China is in the wings and could take over the operation of the Panama Canal at any time. There continues to be an increase in Panamanian property sales to Chinese individuals and companies in and around major cities.

While I stand by everything I said in my congressional testimony in 1999, my views about the U.S. turnover have evolved somewhat in the years since.

People still come up to me and say, "Oh, my God, I can't believe we gave up the Panama Canal." I tell them, "No, it was a good thing." Turning over the canal saved the United States billions of dollars for repairs and the cost of upgrading the locks. Truthfully, the canal had become obsolete for the military and civilian needs of America.

The signing of the treaties also helped to nullify the communist insurgency that had made inroads in Panama and throughout Central America. Before the Panamanians could throw us out, we threw ourselves out and quieted a lot of anti-American sentiment that could have led the U.S. into another costly war to defend the canal.

I don't know if I would have said this in 1999, but I do believe President Jimmy Carter and his administration made a courageous and wise decision signing the Panama Canal treaties. He really knew what was best for America, even though doing so would hurt him politically. Opposition to the treaties was certainly a factor in Carter not being re-elected in 1980. In retrospect, Carter should be recognized for taking an unpopular stand that not only saved the United States a lot of money but, more importantly, saved a lot of lives.

33. Disney

In the first years of my retirement, I occasionally gave presentations on the Panama Canal to community groups. One such engagement in 2004 involved speaking at a library near our home in Florida. At my first talk I gave a 40-minute overview of the canal. That went over so well that I followed it up with a four-part series on the history of Panama, the construction of the canal, canal operations and how a pilot gets a ship through the canal.

I had about 90 people, mostly retirees, who regularly came to the library for these lectures. Always in the front row was a gentleman, a neighbor from my cul-de-sac, who was a retired corporate pilot for Hershey Co. in Pennsylvania.

After a lecture one day, he said to me, "You know, Disney is taking the Disney Magic through the Panama Canal for the first time, from Miami to the West Coast, and they might enjoy these lectures aboard there."

That sounded interesting, but I wasn't sure Disney would be interested. After I retired from the canal, I applied for a job with the Disney Maritime Corp., but I never received a reply. I wasn't sure how I would even approach Disney to be a lecturer on its cruise ships.

Then my neighbor said, "My daughter works for Disney. She's a lawyer. I'll talk to her and have her call you."

Sure enough, a few days later, I got a call, and she told me she would have someone else from Disney get in touch.

Before long, I was invited to Celebration, Florida, where Disney Cruise Lines has its headquarters, to give executives a sample of my lectures. I set up my slideshow – I was just learning PowerPoint – and began my presentation for about 30 Disney employees gathered in a conference room.

I was about 15 minutes into my spiel when an executive stood up and said, "That's it. Fine. Thank you very much, Captain. I think we've seen what we need to see."

With that, I folded up everything, put my laptop in my bag, walked out the door, got in the elevator, went downstairs and began walking to the parking lot. As I got near my car, I heard footsteps and a voice behind me. It was a young secretary who worked for Disney.

"Where are you going?" she asked.

"I'm going home."

"No, please come back here. Disney wants to put you under contract."

Just like that I was signed with Disney, initially on a two-year contract to lecture on its cruise ships during transits of the canal. Over time, I also did a couple of transatlantic cruises with them, too, where I gave presentations on navigating by the stars. I found out most passengers who go on the longer cruises are eager to learn something while having a good time.

As of this writing, Disney's has never taken a ship through the Panama Canal where I haven't been aboard. The company has renewed my contract several times. So, rather than teaching at the university or getting more teaching credentials, I started lecturing on cruises as well as for other interested groups.

Disney Cruise Lines has continued to offer a 14-day "repositioning cruise" through the Panama Canal. Usually in April, the ship heads west through the canal – stopping in several ports during the cruise – to be available for Californian and Alaskan cruises during the spring and summer. In the fall, the ship has returned east through the canal for fall and winter cruises to the Bahamas, the Caribbean and Galveston, Texas.

Originally, the Disney Magic was assigned to go through the canal. Recently, it's been its sister ship, the Disney Wonder, that made the repositioning cruise.

**

After my first Disney transit, other cruise lines started asking me to lecture for them, too. With these other cruise lines, I worked with an agency that places guest lecturers aboard cruise ships on just about any subject.

One time I was hired to give a presentation for eight days aboard the Oasis of the Sea, an 1,865-foot-long cruise ship with a capacity to carry more than 6,000 passengers. The ship is gorgeous, just loaded with amenities, and the crew aboard was extremely nice.

When Darlene and I arrived, the assistant cruise director said to me, "Oh, we're really glad to have you aboard. You can go to your room. Or you and your wife can gamble. Or you can do anything you want. Go ahead, and I'll let you know your schedule."

Right away, Darlene said, "Ken, you're always pretty lucky. Let's go play bingo." Sure enough, I won $500 playing bingo.

The next morning, I said to the cruise director, "Well, what about me getting started here? You got several theaters."

That afternoon, he put me in the ship's sports bar with little notice to passengers. Only three people showed up to hear my presentation on navigation.

I caught up with the cruise director in the afternoon. I said, "Well, I'm doing okay, but – "

He interrupted and said, "You go and have a good time. I'll call you when I need you." The next time I saw him was eight days later when I went down to do an exit briefing.

I said, "I'm really sorry."

He said, "Oh, no. That was fantastic. You did a great job. We want to have you back."

About three weeks later, I got a letter from the vice president of Royal Caribbean saying what a fantastic job I did on the Oasis and they'd like to have me back. I thought: Okay, I won $500 at bingo, I got a free cruise for my wife and me, and all I had to do was lecture one time. I thought: I should do this more often.

Between Disney and other cruise lines, I'm offered enough bookings I could lecture on a different ship each month. As I have gotten older, I've not done that as much as I once did, but I continue to see it as a marvelous way to enjoy my retirement.

***

During my lectures aboard the Disney Magic, I would be talking about a topic and suddenly it would trigger a memory of my experiences in the military or on the canal. I would then launch into a sea story, just off the top of my head.

When I first told the tale of the spider monkey, there were maybe 800 adults and 100 children in the audience. I started saying, "The monkey pooped here" and "The monkey pooped there" and "The monkey was pooping everywhere." And everybody roared with laughter.

Suddenly, in the back of my mind, I thought: I'm on a Disney ship that's totally about family. And I'm using the word "poop." I thought I just blew it. I'm going to lose my job, and I haven't even been here four days. By then it was too late to stop. I finished the story and went on with the lecture.

After I left the stage, the director of all entertainment activities for Disney Cruise Lines came over to me and said, "Captain, I have to talk to you." I thought, uh-oh. Here it comes. She's going to nail me.

She said, "Captain, I got to tell you something. That story about the monkey?"

"Yeah."

"I want you to know that's quite a story. And 'poop' is not a four-letter word with Disney. That's the word kids use. They love 'poop.'"

I thought, oh, God, I dodged a bullet.

I get ready to give a lecture on the Disney Wonder during a fall 2017 cruise through the Panama Canal. (Photo by Rick Thompson.)

***

One of the passengers aboard the Disney ship a few years ago was a woman from Canada, a doctor living in the Arctic Circle with two adopted children. Every eight to ten weeks she was granted a sabbatical, and she'd bring her son and daughter on Disney's Panama Canal cruise.

At the time her son, Rocco, was just 6 years old, but he diligently came to all my lectures, sitting in the front row at every one. Every time I turned around, there was Rocco. So much so, some of the passengers began to think he might be my grandson.

The next year, they were back. And they kept returning for three or four more transits of the canal. They became such regulars that the Disney captain on one transit was kind enough to let me bring Rocco to the ship's bridge. Rocco got to meet the captain and even get his photo taken in the captain's chair.

This experience was one of many instances where I developed strong relationships with passengers when I lectured on a Disney cruise.

I sign autographs for passengers aboard a Panama Canal eastbound cruise on the Disney Wonder in fall 2017. (Photo by Rick Thompson.)

***

On my second Disney cruise, a woman asked, "How do they keep ships from running into each other at night?" I proceeded to explain that ships use radar and other sophisticated electronics, but they didn't have those in the old days. Sailing ships sent signals to other vessels using colored lights. A red light was placed to show the port (left) side. A green light was on the starboard (right) side. White lights were placed high to show the distance the ship was from other vessels.

When I was a pilot, because I knew ship captains were always a bit nervous going through the Panama Canal, I would sometimes go aboard wearing a red sock on my left foot and a green one on my other. I'd tell the captain I wore different colors to keep track of which side was port and which was starboard. It always got a big laugh, and people would relax a bit.

Remembering that, aboard the second Disney cruise I wore a red sock on my left foot and a green one on my right. I didn't say anything about it the first day. But I could tell some people spotted them and thought perhaps I was color blind. The next lecture I again wore the red and green socks, and then finally told the story. Since it got a good laugh, I've made it a part of all my lectures. I did it in hopes people would think to themselves: Maybe this lecture series won't be as boring as we thought it might be.

***

I guess about 75 percent of the passengers on one of Disney's Panama Canal transits are older couples and retirees. They aren't aboard just to see the shows, visit ports and have great meals. They made a point to book a Panama Canal transit because they wanted to learn about this historic and technological marvel, and they see my lectures as a way to enhance the experience.

When I'm on a Disney cruise, I don't just give lectures to the adult passengers. I'm frequently asked to talk separately to the youngsters as part of their homeschooling.

Sometimes, I also give a presentation to the crew in their lounge on a lower deck. They, too, are often going through the Panama Canal for the first time.

Exploring the crew area on the Disney ships is like visiting another world altogether. The main corridor runs from the bow to the stern, right in the middle of the ship. It's called Highway 95, after the name of the East Coast's main interstate. There is a laundry, supply rooms, storerooms, galleys and crew quarters for about 900 people. Crew members work six hours on, six off, or eight on, eight off, so I interact with them a lot.

***

On the first day of a Disney cruise, after I do a rehearsal in the theater, I am free for the afternoon and evening. My wife and I like to be on the top deck for Disney's spectacular sail-away party at 4 p.m.

For a lot of passengers, one thrill of a Disney cruise is when they are leaving port and the ship's loud whistle sounds the tune "When You

Passengers aboard the Disney Wonder celebrate at a sail-away party in April 2017 as the ship was leaving Port Canaveral on a 14-day cruise that would take it through the Panama Canal. (Photo by William LaRue.)

Wish Upon a Star." The guests probably don't know that Disney had to go to the U.S. Coast Guard and the international maritime community to get special permission to install that whistle signal. Similarly, when it ordered its first cruise ship, Disney approached the international maritime authorities for permission to paint the lifeboats a different color. The regulation color is orange. Disney was permitted to paint lifeboats yellow in a shade that's similar to the color of Mickey Mouse's shoes.

Disney often wins exceptions because, well, it is Disney.

34. Historic Disney cruise

DARLENE and I were aboard the Disney Wonder when it made a bit of history on Saturday, April 29, 2017, by becoming the first cruise ship to pass through the newly expanded locks of the Panama Canal,

When I first heard the Wonder was going through the new locks, I wondered how they were going to pull off the transit without damage to this beautiful ship. Unlike the older locks, the new ones don't use locomotives with cables to help keep ships in the middle of the chambers. Instead, ships typically are tied up against rubber-like fenders on the walls while recycled lake water flows into the chambers from side basins to raise the vessels. That's fine for a cargo ship or tanker that can expect a few dings and dents. But if you lay a cruise ship along a concrete wall and drag it like you do cargo ships, you're going to tear the heck out of it. You'll mess the whole side up.

During shipyard renovation of the Disney Wonder in 2016, they added what is known in the maritime industry as the "duck tail." It is an extension to the stern that makes the vessel more stable and is thought to increase speed. This extension increased the length of the Wonder to 984 feet, which meant it no longer could fit safely through the old Panama lock system.

It didn't surprise me that a Disney ship would be the first to go through the new locks. Disney likes to be first. Disney may even have negotiated a special deal to be the first through the new locks. Personally, I wouldn't have wanted to be first. I might have wanted to see how the canal handled other cruise ships.

The Disney Wonder becomes the first cruise ship to transit the Panama Canal's Cocoli Locks on its way to the Pacific Ocean on April 29, 2017. (Photo by EFE/Alejandro Boliver.)

On April 29, like many passengers, Darlene and I were up before 5 a.m. while darkness still enveloped the ship. I always get a bit of "channel fever" on the day of a transit. Just coming into port wakes me up. It's a condition every sailor experiences. Most people on this cruise day are up before sunrise because they know they are about to take part in something special.

In the past, I've often been allowed to watch transits from the bridge. Due to increased security, this is no longer allowed on any ship. During the spring 2017 transit on the Wonder, Darlene and I camped out in the exercise room, which is a great spot to witness a crossing. It's at the front of the ship just one deck below the wheelhouse. It's air-conditioned. There's a place to sit down. You're not outside in the heat. If it's raining, you don't get wet.

After finding a nice quiet spot, I turned on a portable radio that tuned in communications between the ship and the canal authorities. I couldn't transmit, but I could listen.

***

5:30 a.m. The ship, under the command of Captain Robert Olmer, eased past the breakwater in the Caribbean side of the Panama Canal. We arrived right at our appointed time. A ship doesn't just show up to go through the canal. It has to give 96 hours' notice beforehand. And all tolls must be paid in advance. I'm not certain how much Disney paid in tolls for the Wonder to transit the new locks. The company treats that information as confidential. But based on what I know about the fees, it was somewhere around $500,000. That included an extra 10 percent on top of the regular tolls for priority transit.

By now, many passengers were turning on their TV sets for the lively daily preview show hosted by cruise director Darren McBurney and his assistant, Anthony Youngblut.

Darren: This is it, folks. Today is the day we've been building up to for the first half of the voyage. … You're going to be able to say you were one of the 1,856, I think, guests onboard, or the 2,800 with the crew as well, that went through the locks first. … We are estimating going through that first lock this morning, nice and early, around 7:30 a.m.

Anthony: Get up. Get out.

Darren: At the end of the day, at the final lock at the opposite end, our estimated arrival is around 2:10 p.m. and we'll leave that lock at 4:40 p.m.

Anthony: That's very precise, Darren.

Darren: I know. We're trying to be as precise as possible. But we're going to keep you updated throughout the day as well.

Now, folks, as we said, it's all going to be happening out on the deck, and it's just a day to watch, first of all, the natural beauty you're going to see at certain points in the day, but also that experience of going through these brand-new locks.

Anthony: And I think everybody knows a lot of it already because they've all been watching Captain Ken Puckett.

Darren: They have been watching Captain Ken, and he's been keeping you well-informed. And definitely at the same time entertained as well.

Anthony: He's got like two different colored socks and stuff like that.

Darren: Everything. Everything.

***

6 a.m. There is a speed limit as we approached the canal. The Wonder couldn't come through there at 12 miles an hour. The ship had to proceed at 3 or 4 miles an hour. Otherwise, it would be going too fast for pilots to board.

Before long, a launch pulled alongside. The first control pilot came aboard with two trainees. We picked up two more pilots before we arrived at the entrance to Agua Clara Locks, part of the newly expanded section of the canal. The additional pilots were stationed where they could monitor parts of the canal that were out of sight of the control pilot.

As we moved nearer to the locks, more launches arrived. They carried ship's agents, boarding officers, security officers and two crews assigned to handle tug lines.

Of course, lots of paperwork had to be processed before the ship could go through. Even though this is the age of computers and electronic communications, some actions still require paper. Documents still need to be signed.

Four tugboats soon arrived alongside the ship, twice the number I had when using the older locks for cruise ships. Having four tugboats adds cost to a transit, which is one reason tolls have increased. However, two extra tugboats do make a transit safer. These are very, very large, 12,000- to 15,000-horsepower tugboats with lots of power to control the ship.

Just before we reached Agua Clara, a narrator, Ed Paulk, came aboard. A former Panama Canal Commission public relations executive, he was hired by Disney's agent in Panama to describe for passengers what they were seeing. His narration was transmitted by loudspeakers on the top deck and over the TV sets in passengers' rooms.

I have been on other cruise ships where they said, "We got Ken Puckett aboard. He's going to do the narration." But No. 1, that's not in my contract and, No. 2, I don't want to take this job away from somebody else. So, I don't do the narration unless it's necessary. When I've done it, it makes for a long day.

***

7:30 a.m. A brisk wind of maybe 16 knots was blowing out of the northeast as we reached the first set of locks. By now hundreds of passengers had gathered on the top deck, where Disney laid out tables with complimentary coffee, tea, muffins and other refreshments.

An announcement was made over the P.A. system warning passengers on the front of the top deck that they might want to cover their ears. Then the ship's whistle let loose with a mighty blast of "When You Wish Upon a Star" to a bevy of cheers.

The first gates opened, and the Wonder and two tugboats entered the first chamber. Then to my surprise, crews didn't tie up the Wonder to a wall.

Ed Paulk commented on this change in standard procedure.

"So, we start making our entrance," he said. "Normally they have a crew standing by on the wall. Normally they would lean it up against the wall and tie it to the wall. They're going to try something a little bit different. They're going to try to keep it right in the center of the chamber. No lines or anything."

Then to my further surprise, the side basins that recycle water weren't used – a decision, I assume, that was made to minimize the turbulence of water pouring in from left to right. Instead, canal workers gently allowed water to flow from the upper chambers down to ones below to lift the ship, just like the process used on the older locks.

It sounded from Ed's narration that he was surprised, too. "Okay, as far as the water-saving basins – and we are directly to the right of those – they are not going to use them. They are not going to use them."

Kept away from the walls by tugboats and the ship's thrusters, the Wonder made it through the locks without a scratch. If the canal had tried to take the ship through that way during a bad storm with 20 to 30 knots of wind blowing, the Wonder likely would have jackknifed, gone onto the wall and it would have been a real mess. But the weather was just perfect as far as wind goes. The Wonder stayed right in the middle of the chambers.

Of course, there was a huge waste of water to skip using the basins. Instead of 30 million gallons of lake water to go through the first set of locks, they used about 70 million for the Wonder. But it seems to me it was worth it to keep that delicate ship off the wall.

Down below I could see passengers busily shooting videos and photographs. Above the ship, I spotted a drone darting around, capturing video of its own. There also were lots of cameras along the canal where people waved and snapped pictures. It's always a big deal in Panama when a Disney ship goes through – but being the first passenger ship through the new locks, it was getting even more attention than usual.

In his continued narration, Ed Paulk captured the celebratory mood of the transit: "We do have some photographers on the gate. Photographers everywhere. This is kind of a big day. It really is very exciting. It's quite an honor also. For months and months, there was all kinds of talk which would be the first – I've been on some of the other cruise ships – and they'd say, 'Well, who's going to be the first?' And all of that. And here we are today. It's an exciting moment."

***

10 a.m. The Wonder departed Agua Clara and began making its slow trek across Gatun Lake. For the next few hours, the transit was routine, perhaps even boring. A lot of other people must have thought the same thing; when Darlene and I went to breakfast, a lot of others left the top decks and joined us.

Because I had given several lectures already on this cruise, people came by to visit and ask questions. A common one was: "Can people drink the lake water?" The short answer is no. Twenty years ago, the water was fresh enough you could bring it aboard a ship and drink it. But since then they've polluted it. And that terrible smell some passengers noticed when we were on the Atlantic side? That was from a garbage dump that's been burning for 14 years.

Welcome to 21st century Panama.

***

11:20 a.m. We passed Gamboa, the port that's the midway point of the Panama Canal. It's also the beginning point where a ditch goes through the Continental Divide at the mouth of the Chagres River. Darlene and I returned to our spot in the exercise room.

On the lake we passed numerous other ships. About ten ships a day go through the new lock system, usually five each way, plus traffic through the old locks. There were also a lot of ships anchored in the lake waiting to make a night transit.

***

12:10 p.m. The ship cleared Gamboa. Up to now, it had been a nice day, not too warm due to the overcast skies. But now a light rain began to fall, and we were pleased to be inside where it was dry. Disney passed out free plastic ponchos to the dwindling number of passengers who continued to stand outside along the rails. Panama's dry season begins officially on December 15 and ends April 15, so the rain was pretty much on schedule.

Passengers on the Disney Wonder endure light rain during its Panama Canal transit in spring 2017. (Photo by William LaRue.)

Over the P.A. system, Ed Paulk continued to blend observations of the sights with a bit of history about Panama's notorious landslides in what is now called the Culebra Cut.

"There's another pretty good example on our right of material breaking away, including a humongous boulder. I guess eventually they'll fill it up with dynamite and blow it up," Ed told the passengers. "So, this Cut – 8 miles long – is an engineers' nightmare. We've had two-dozen major slides. ... The last one occurred the 13th of October of 1986. It slid straight across but only to the middle. In the middle, it stopped. So, in other words, it did not block traffic. But it did make it a little bit slower because it was one-way through that area."

***

2:10 p.m. The Disney Wonder arrived at Cocoli Locks on the Pacific side of the canal.

***

4:40 p.m. We departed the last set of locks following a lengthy onboard ceremony attended by executives for the Panama Canal Authority and Disney Cruise Lines celebrating the historic transit. The president of the cruise lines even flew to Panama to get a document for the occasion, have his photo taken and shake a lot of hands. Not long afterward, the onboard narration went silent as Ed said goodbye and departed.

***

5:10 p.m. The Disney Wonder passed under the Bridge of the Americas and headed for a refueling spot before continuing north toward our eventual destination in San Diego a week later.

Two plaques, presented to the Disney Wonder, are put on display in glass case on the ship after it became the first passenger ship to transit the newly expanded locks of the Panama Canal. The plaque on the left reads: "Canal de Panama. The Great Connection. Maiden Transit. M/V Disney Wonder on the occasion of First Transit through the Neopanamax Locks. 2017." The one on the right reads: "Disney Wonder. The first cruise ship to transit Panama Canal's new locks. April 29, 2017. Presented by Inchcape Shipping Services – Panama. Proud to be supporting Disney Cruise Line in Panama since 2005." Inchcape is Disney's agent in Panama. (Photo by William LaRue.)

Despite a little rain and a brief delay due to the celebration, it was a very good transit. The pilots did a fine job under a lot of pressure. And I give credit, too, to the tugboat captains and the captain and crew of the Disney ship for making it all work so seamlessly that most passengers probably weren't aware of the change in locks procedures.

At my lecture the next morning, I informed the audience that a big storm was pummeling Panama as I spoke. Had it hit a day earlier, we undoubtedly would have tied up along the wall and come away with a few bruises to show for it.

Speaking of wear and tear, my voice did not survive the cruise unscathed. Before we reached San Diego, I explained during a lecture that I made a visit the night before to the ship's dispensary, where a doctor sprayed something in my throat to take care of the hoarseness.

Of course, a slight sore throat has never stopped me on cruises from sharing my sea stories – or from looking forward to my next gig. "I do weddings, bar mitzvahs," I joked. "If you got anything you want me to do, let me know."

When the laughter quieted, I acknowledged there might be a method to my madness, a philosophy of life learned long ago. "If you act a little crazy," I said, "nobody bothers you."

Epilogue

OVER the years, I have been battling numerous health problems related to my exposure to Agent Orange in Vietnam. I am not alone in this struggle. Thousands of Americans who served in Vietnam, as well as countless numbers of Vietnamese, have suffered because of the U.S. military's use of that defoliant. Unfortunately, many veterans fail to obtain their entitled treatments and benefits. Thus, I spend part of my time these days advising Florida residents on these issues, even as the Veterans Administration continues to identify new illnesses linked to Agent Orange.

I have had the good fortune in retirement to continue to share my canal experiences on cruise ships and interacting with the passengers. I've now been lecturing for about as many years as I was a pilot on the canal. This has helped me to stay connected with a job I loved. I miss ship-handling. I really do.

In the process of putting together this book with co-author and longtime journalist William LaRue, I've encountered through his research details of my history that had been unknown to me. For example, I only recently learned what happened to my stepfather, Clarence Combs, after he abandoned our family. Records from the internet revealed that he married at least twice after leaving my mother. He died in July 1968, in Orange County, California.

My biological father, George Archey, died in March 1986 in Tennessee. Although we never spoke again after my visit to Rockwood in the 1960s, I remained in touch with one of his sons who lives in Florida and one of George Archey's grandsons in Tennessee. George

Archey's widow, Mayble, the kind woman who offered to raise me as her son, died in August 2011.

My mother died in February 1985. She was only 64. In the research for this book, I was stunned to learn of an incident in her life that she kept secret from me – further proof that, even with close family, you don't always know them as much as you thought you did,

Two news articles from the 1930s when she was 16 years old reveal how Mom and another girl were victims of a terrifying attack on a back road of Kentucky.

The Cincinnati Enquirer on March 25, 1937, first reported the story under the headline "Two Men Sought By Police On Girls' Charges of Attempted Assault; Young Women Left on Highway to Walk."

The article reads:

"Two Newport men were being sought early this morning by Campbell County police after two young women told Newport police of an attempted attack on a lonely country road near Butler, Ky., 30 miles south of Newport.

"Victims of the attempted attack were Miss Kathryn Simms, 19 years old, 715 Garrard Street, Covington, and Miss Vernice Vogt, 16, Cold Spring, Ky.

"According to the story they told Sergeant Kenneth Collins of Newport police, the girls took a ride with the two men, planning to attend a dance. Miss Vogt said she met the men at Eleventh and Brighton Streets, Newport, last night. She said they asked her to accompany them to the home of Miss Simms after which they would go to the dance.

"Reaching Butler, the driver of the automobile, the girl said, began making advances, which they resisted.

"After the girls had been pushed from the car, the men then jumped into it and drove away, leaving the girls in the middle of the road.

"While (they were) walking toward Newport a passing motorist, who said his name was Vernon Fisher, Chattanooga, Tenn., saw the girls and offered to take them back to Newport. Fisher said he was on his way to Chattanooga at the time.

"The trio arrived at police headquarters shortly before 1 o'clock this morning. Because the attempted attack occurred outside the city limits of Newport, County Patrolman Harry Rosenhagen and Albert Gerhardt were called in to investigate the case.

"Except for scratched hands and rumpled clothing, the girls were not harmed, they said.

"Before meeting Fisher, the girls said, they had been walking along the highway for an hour and a half."

Two days later, the *Enquirer* reported that two suspects, Willie Shields and George Thomas, both 22, had been arrested and charged – not with assault or attempted assault but with breach of the peace. A judge fined them the "costs of court" and placed both on probation for six months. It is hard to imagine that the court system even in those days would treat so lightly a case involving two grown men accused of trying to force themselves on a couple of teenagers, leaving them scratched and rumpled, pushing them out of a car, and abandoning them along a country road.

After learning about this incident, I spoke with a cousin who knew about it and disclosed to me how little sympathy my mother had gotten from the community after the men were arrested. How traumatic it must have been for Mom to go through the assault, then be wounded all over again by the community giving her a hard time.

I understand why she felt it necessary to keep this secret, but I wish I had known while she was still alive. It's been a struggle for me to work through this knowledge. Perhaps I would have been more sympathetic and understanding, certainly less bitter of her behavior toward my siblings and me. I understand as well as anyone how difficult it is to recover when things go so badly when you're young.

My half-brother, Ronald Puckett, died in January 2011. After graduating from high school, Ron served with the U.S. Air Force for eight years. He was a man of many interests, particularly sports. He rooted for the Cincinnati Reds and Cleveland Browns. He loved to bowl and to umpire for Little League. He even co-hosted a radio show, "Rowdy Ron and Mean Gene," on WAIF-FM in Kentucky. Over the years, Ron reconnected with the family of his biological father, Nute Puckett. When Ron died, he was buried in the Puckett family cemetery in Clay County, Kentucky, his obituary noting "his final wish to be buried next to his father."

As for my surviving family, I remain very close with my half-sister, Barbara, and her family.

My stepson, Chad, is a senior computer engineer in San Antonio, Texas. He has three children, Lauren, Lucy and Cole.

My stepdaughter, Wendy, works in community outreach at the Village Library in Granville, Ohio. Her husband, Ed, is database administrator for an executive charter-jet company. They have three children, Brendan, Kelsey and Jacob.

My son, Ken, worked for 12 years on the Columbia River, and he rose from a deckhand to dual status as riverboat captain and chief engineer. In 2004, he left the maritime industry. Today, he is vice president of operations for the MSL Timbers Soccer Club in Portland, Oregon.

My daughter, Karen, is a program manager with the Federal Aviation Administration in Seattle, Washington. She has two children, Lexi and Nick.

Nick has chosen to follow in my military footsteps. He entered the U.S. Navy in early 2016 and graduated from the Naval Training Center in Great Lakes, Illinois. It was additionally memorable for me because he graduated on that same date in June that I graduated from there exactly 58 years earlier. I attended Nick's graduation with Karen and her fiancé, David, and I wore my official uniform as Nick requested. He is currently a Navy third-class petty officer-naval electronic aviation specialist, working on Navy helicopters in San Diego.

Of course, I found a perfect partner in my marriage to Darlene, who has kept me grounded for these past 29 years, even when we're at sea. As I recently told passengers during one of my cruise lectures, "My wife is hiding out there in the audience somewhere checking on my programs and monitoring my sea stories." She is my editor, mentor and keeps me on an even course. I may be a captain on the ship, but she is the captain at home. And she is the best!

I'm also grateful to my ex-wife, Shirley, and to our children, Karen and Ken, for hanging in there for me while I was in the military and afterward. Like most military families, my career also put them into military service. During their time we were together, we moved across the ocean twice, across the United States six times, and lived in eight military housing units. I know it took a toll on them. But they never complained – or, if they did, I didn't hear it.

A couple of years ago, I happened to have one of my old military hats on the dash in the car. A man at a car wash asked me, "Are you still in the military?" Before I could answer, he added, "You seem awfully old to be in the service."

I thought about that for a second and replied, "I don't think I really ever left. It's still a part of who I am."

At the end of the Vietnam War, many veterans and their families weren't always treated well by our nation. Fortunately, the U.S. military is doing a much better job these days of supporting military families. And the country as a whole has come to better respect the service and sacrifices of our military men, women and their families. I pray this support is something that never goes away.

All in all, despite a few stormy times, I've enjoyed what my daughter, Karen, likes to call my "Puckett luck."

Perhaps the best example of this was my good fortune to be taken under the wing of Army Chief Warrant Officer Carter C. James after I transferred from the Navy in the 1960s. Somehow, Mr. James took a liking to me. He likely saw in me a reflection of himself, including parallels to his previous service in the Navy. After we met a few times, he said to me, "Ken, we are a lot alike, you and me." He generously offered to be my mentor and manage my career.

Over the next 12 years that I was in the Army, I worked directly for him three times, and he made sure my other assignments were career-oriented. I'm positive that Mr. James was directly responsible for my assignment to the Maritime College. We were a team.

We kept in touch after I left the Army, and he was there to encourage me to apply to be a pilot on the Panama Canal. He once noted that I was the only person he knew who had worked as a ship pilot in four countries: Vietnam, Japan, South Korea and Panama.

Not long before Mr. James passed away in 2016, I visited him in Virginia. He said something to me then that I've treasured since: "Ken, I just want you to know how proud I am of you."

Mr. James was my boss, a mentor and a friend. But he was more than that, too. He truly was the father I never really had.

Over the years, I learned much from Mr. James and others. No lesson was more important than trying to have a good attitude. I used to tell troops under me, "If you make a mistake but you tried your best and had a good attitude, I won't come down hard on you."

Sometimes in life, you make mistakes. Things do go bad. But you learn to roll with it. Don't internalize it. It just holds you down.

No matter how dark things seem, one thing is certain: The sun does come up every day.

About the authors

Kᴇɴɴᴇᴛʜ P. Puckett, a native of Kentucky and a retired ship pilot on the Panama Canal, joined the U.S Navy in 1958. He spent the next eight years mostly on sea duty aboard submarines, destroyers and an aircraft carrier. In 1966, he transferred to the U.S. Army, where he rose to the rank of chief warrant officer. He served in the Army in postings that included Vietnam, Okinawa and South Korea. In 1972, he was placed on independent duty and assigned to New York State Maritime College, Bronx, New York, where he graduated in 1974 with a bachelor's degree in marine transportation. He retired from the Army in 1978 after 20 years of military service.

In 1980, Captain Puckett was selected by the Panama Canal Commission to join its elite corps of ship pilots. He worked for nearly 16 years in Panama, including stints as a senior pilot and a port captain. During that time, he safely piloted over a thousand vessels on the

Panama Canal. In 1992, he received the Panama Canal's Outstanding Employee of the Year Award. In 1993, he was awarded the Panama Canal Commission's Silver Medal for Public Service for his work as an alcohol and drug counselor. He retired from the canal in 1996.

Since then, Captain Puckett, who now lives in Florida with his wife, Darlene, has developed a series of lectures on the Panama Canal and maritime history. He routinely presents these lectures aboard the luxury cruise ships of Carnival UK, Cunard, Disney, Princess, Royal Caribbean and Yachts of Seabourn.

William D. LaRue lives with his wife, Kathleen, in Liverpool, New York, where they raised two children. He is an award-winning journalist, former TV critic for *The Post-Standard* in Syracuse, New York, and is currently a website producer for several major newspapers. William received a bachelor's degree in English from SUNY Potsdam and a master's degree in communications from Syracuse University. He is the author of the 1999 book *Collecting Simpsons!* and the co-author of his late father's 2015 memoirs, *CANDY: True Tales of a 1st Cavalry Soldier in the Korean War and Occupied Japan*.

Made in the
USA
Lexington, KY